THE GATE
BEHIND THE
WALL

A Pilgrimage to Jerusalem

Samuel Heilman

SUMMIT BOOKS

NEW YORK

10 9 8 7 6 5 4 3 2 1

Library of Congress Cataloging in Publication Data
Heilman, Samuel C.
    The gate behind the wall.
    1. Orthodox Judaism—Jerusalem. 2. Talmud
Torah (Judaism) 3. Heilman, Samuel C. 4. Jews—
Jerusalem—Social life and customs. 5. Jerusalem—
Social life and customs. I. Title.
BM392.J4H44 1984   296.8′32′0956944   84-8659
ISBN 0-671-52489-5

For Chaya Glikeh bat Yechiel Yaakov
May her memory be a blessing

CONTENTS

I hold that each man has a self, and enlarges his self by his experiences. That is, he learns from experience: from the experiences of others as well as his own, and from their inner experiences as well as their outer. But he can learn from their inner experience only by entering it, and that is not done merely by reading a written record of it. We must have the gift to identify ourselves with other men, to relive their experience.

J. Bronowski

Study the Torah again and again, for everything is contained in it; constantly examine it, grow old and gray over it, and swerve not from it, for there is nothing more excellent than it.

Ben Bag-Bag

PROLOGUE

Generation after generation, the Jewish people have repeated a story, recounting events that took place nearly two thousand years ago, when around the city of Jerusalem, in which the Holy Temple stood, Roman legions camped and laid a siege from which the Jews could not escape. Some Jews, the zealots, or *biryoni*, looked upon this siege as opportunity. They would not wait the months and years the full stores of food allowed and set about at once to prepare for a battle they fully believed they could win. They burned the stores, in hopes that by that act the spirits of their fellows would be fired to bring about the glorious war in which the pious few could triumph over the mighty infidel. The Holy Temple would never fall; Jerusalem would stand forever.

Within the city was a man—Rabbi Yochanan ben Zakkai—who did not share this vision. He looked upon the *biryoni* as too much attached to earth and stone. For him the Temple, holy as it was, had already fallen; the Jerusalem of this world was on the edge of ruin. For his people to ascend from it, another gateway had to be found. But first he had to find a way out of the earthly city. At every gate *biryoni* stood guard. They meant to keep everyone inside until the moment when fighting would erupt. Only the dead would be allowed to leave—for they had other places they could go.

"Take me out as a dead man," the rabbi said to his students. The word went out that the great sage had become ill, had grown worse, had died.

And when all Jerusalem thought the sage was gone, he called his students together and asked them to place him inside a casket. Eliezer, his greatest disciple, lifted his head while Yehoshua, another student, took his feet, and thus they carried him through the streets until at sunset they reached the gate behind the city wall.

"What is this?" asked Abba Sikra, leader of the zealots who barred the way.

"A dead man who is going to another world," the students answered. And then they added: "You know well the law that the dead may not be buried inside the city."

But the *biryoni* wanted to run their spears through the body to make certain the man was dead.

"Here lies the great sage Rabbi Yochanan ben Zakkai!" the students cried out. "Would you so dishonor the remains of such a man?"

So Abba Sikra relented and the gates were cracked open. Thus, Eliezer and Yehoshua carried the casket until they came near the camp of the Roman legion and its commander, Vespasian. There at last they opened the box. The rabbi arose and stood before the Roman.

"Hail and peace, O Emperor!" he greeted him. And as Vespasian watched the "dead" man come to life, the rabbi repeated his greeting: "Hail and peace, O Emperor!"

"I am not Emperor," Vespasian answered.

"But you shall be," the rabbi said, "for no one but a king could hope to conquer Jerusalem."

As they spoke, a messenger approached from Rome and told Vespasian their Emperor was dead and Rome decreed that he must lead the nation.

There is some dispute in Jewish tradition about what happened next, about who spoke and what was said. In every version of the tale, however, the conclusion is the same: Vespasian turned to the rabbi and said, "I leave from here and there shall come another who will take my place to lay this siege. But since you were the first who saw for me what I had not yet seen, I shall reward you with a single wish. What will it be?"

Again there is dispute about what next was said and what requested, what could be got and what could not. But in the end, as all agree, one plea was made and not rejected: "Give me Yavneh and its scholars."

Behind lay earth-and-stone Jerusalem, the one to which Abba Sikra and the *biryoni* had attached themselves. Its Temple could be burned, its holy vessels carried off, its inner sanctum desecrated. Not too far away in that same holy land sat Yavneh, a settlement in which dwelt men who plumbed the depths of Scripture and of God's law, and here another temple was being built. But this was not a temple of the earthly regions; it was one in which the scholar was the priest, in which true service came through study, in which the Torah was the holy of holies. Here, the rabbi felt, the future Jerusalem lay.

The Temple fell, and earthly Jerusalem burned. The *biryoni* fought and lost. Some ran into the desert, to Masada, where once again the few would face the many and once again would lose. But the path Yochanan ben Zakkai had opened was still being traveled. Since his time, the road between the two Jerusalems had passed, for many Jews, through texts—between the lines of black on white, around the Scriptures and their Talmudic interpretation. The Temple now was portable; the stones were words, the walls ideas—and nothing could destroy them.

Wherever groups of Jews gathered, they found their Yavneh and built their temple by forming a study circle—a *chavruse*, as it was called. And thus they reconstructed lost Jerusalem.

The great sage Rav said—and some say it was Rabbi Shmuel bar Marta: "Greater is the study of Torah than the building of the Holy Temple."

INTRODUCTION

The Old Shall Be Made New;
The New Shall Be Made Holy

I live in two worlds and have done so as long as I can remember. In one, I am attached to an eternal yesterday—a timeless faith and ritual, an ancient system of behavior. In that world, I am an Orthodox Jew. In my other world, there is little if any attachment to the enchantment of religion or sacred practice, and what is happening today or tomorrow matters far more than the verities embedded in the past. In that domain, I am a university professor of sociology.

To live in these opposing spheres I have often found it necessary to divide myself, placing different aspects of my character in different compartments. On Friday nights and Sabbaths, during my daily prayers, in my home with my family, through the food that I eat and inside the synagogue, I have been attached to the Judaism of past generations, guiding my life by the strictest rules of behavior and belief. At other times and in other places, I have transformed myself into a modern man who tries to be a part of the contemporary society around him.

In order to carry on this double life, I find myself trying at times to forget one side of my identity while playing my other parts. Without this selective memory, this capacity to dim the lights in one room while I am in the other, I would have to teeter precariously on the edge of estrangement, never feeling quite at home in either of my two worlds.

I have thought at times of abandoning one of my two worlds in favor of the other, to be at last at one with myself. But each time I think of doing so, I recall the famous parable of the dove who, feeling the resistance of the wind in his feathers, dreamed he would fly better in a vacuum. And then I realize that for me there can be no such flight. Besides, I realize that each world has become more attractive to me by the possibility of life in the other.

Yet if for me compartmentalization is possible and sometimes even desirable, it is far from satisfying, for it forces upon me a kind of abiding denial of parts of my self, a walling up of experience and existence. So I, like many other modern Orthodox Jews, people who move between religious tradition and the secular present, have tried wherever possible to collapse the boundaries between these two worlds and find a way to make myself whole. This is the story of such an effort.

"Nu," as he looked at me, my local rabbi asked, "are you *lernen* at all? Do you ever pick up a *Gemara?"* He tapped the open volume of Talmud that he held in his hand as he spoke.

I shrugged my shoulders. For months since my move to his suburban New York community, he had been asking me this question at least every other week. Every time he reminded me of my Jewish obligation to *lern,* to ritually review the Talmud, I thought only of a book filled with archaic legalisms, implausible stories and arcane rabbinic debates that had never been able to capture my imagination.

Although we worshiped in the same place, the rabbi was not like me. However much he entered into contemporary life and values, he still could open up a holy book and spend his hours *lernen*, during which he turned away from present-day America and let himself pass into another time and place in which tradition was the master, in which the unrelenting past still reigned. Because he loved to wander in that tradition, he often sat beside the wall of the synagogue while waiting for his congregation to assemble for prayers and quietly read through a page of Talmud or some rabbinic commentary. And every now and then, if I was there early and waiting too, he'd call me over and try to take me with him through a piece of text. But while I sat with him and tried to follow along, more often than not I found the words blurring before my eyes and my mind wandering off to some other place and time.

For nearly a year I always answered his recurrent inquiry with a shrug. The rabbi knew that my world was the university, my special interest sociology, and that into this way of life the Talmud did not easily fit. Each time he asked his question, he'd look piercingly and unblinkingly into my eyes for just a moment, then finally shrug too and turn back to the book which, always open, lay there between us.

Throughout my years in the precincts of modern Orthodoxy, where people strive in principle to remain committed to the strictures of observant Judaism while remaining neither remote from nor untouched by contemporary society, I have been taught that however archaic various aspects of Jewish life and observance might seem, they can all be understood in ways that would make them sparkle in the light of contemporary life. There is nothing so old that it cannot be made part of the modern world, no tradition so ancient that it could not be made a living part of contemporary reality. The old can be made new.

Not only that, but the modern world is not so radically new that one could not find its reflection in the past. The new can be made holy.

The task of reconciling the old and the new has not been easy. Few rabbis or religious leaders I found around me could or would help. The norm has seemed to me to be "Every man for himself"; and so I have slowly—not always successfully— been weaving my way between modernity and Orthodoxy, try- ing to find a way to make of my life a single tapestry. But in that fabric, an important Jewish thread, one that ran through thou- sands of years of my people's history, was for a long time still missing. I had not found a way to study Torah.

Of all that Judaism values, nothing is more highly treasured than the study of Torah, the great sacred literature whose core is the Bible and whose mantle is the Talmud.

Talmud. In Hebrew, the word means "study," the teachings that one acquires from his predecessors. But the Talmud is more: a multivolumed compilation of ancient rabbinic debate and commentary—the *Gemara*—about an oral tradition—the *Mishna*—which the faithful believe was first revealed at Sinai. Filled with narrative and legal disputation, it is a somewhat cryptic and not altogether systematic record of oral discussions that took place in the first-century academies of Jewish learning in Palestine and later, between the third and fifth centuries, in Babylonia, which, following the exile, became the new center of diaspora Jewish life. There, scholars reviewed the legal path- ways of Jewish life—the *halacha*—while they explored custom, belief, folkways and history through homily and narrative—the *aggada*. And over the centuries since then, Jews have tried to repeat that process. At home, in the synagogue study hall—the *bes medresh*—in the academy of Jewish learning—the *yeshiva*

—they would gather to recite and review the Talmud, the great repository of rabbinic and Jewish wisdom.

Since the Talmud contains not only rabbinic discussion but also citations of Scripture, laws and legends, review of it can be said to subsume all of Jewish sacred literature. It rests upon and above all other holy books. And those scholars who have deciphered its logic and fathomed its wisdom likewise sit at the pinnacle of Jewish learning.

I was never one of those scholars. Unlike many Orthodox Jews, I could not luxuriate inside a page of Talmud or rabbinic commentary. Nor could I connect with its logic or see beyond its apparently parochial concerns. The arguments it put forth and the situations it described had always seemed too far away from the world I inhabited and the concerns in my life. To join with others in the review of a most sacred Jewish text, the great Oral Law, the Talmud was something unappealing. The text's concern with the minutiae of law, its telegraphic style and tortured prose, the complicated and often unbelievable legends and endless reinterpretations of ancient Biblical verses had never worked their magic on me. Scriptures were important—and I had long ago learned to appreciate at least their narrative portions and homilies—but throughout my years as a young boy in the *yeshiva*, I had found Talmud opaque at best and sometimes even boring. I simply could not understand its appeal for so many of my fellow Jews, both present and past.

Many of those Jews still inhabit parts of the Orthodox world in which I dwell. For them, what is often called in the Yiddish vernacular *"lernen"*—a term freighted with Jewish history and attachments to living sacred texts—has always appeared to me to be a gate whereby they enter the life of piety and awe. These are people who come to the holy books not so much to exercise their intellect as to express their devotion and attachment to a God whose revealed word they believe the books contain. These traditionalists have always seemed able—at least temporarily—to find ways of escaping the claims of modernity by involving themselves in Talmud. For them the best questions are those the tradition has already asked and answered, and the most touching narratives are those everyone already knows. For them, the past is master.

Although I could not bring myself to join these people who plant themselves around a holy text, I knew—and was reminded by those around me who celebrate the traditional Orthodox Jewish way of life and *lernen*—the review of the holy words and ancient ideas is, after all, an activity associated with the heart of my religion. My earliest memories were of a Jewish world where prayer was a daily occurrence and where the Torah—the central organizing element of our religion—and all it symbolized remained the single most important source of illumination. Throughout my life, therefore, I believed I had to wait until I would be ready to penetrate that experience.

In the meantime, however, I entered the university and found another way of life to embrace. Charmed by the cultural riches of Western civilization and its spirit of free inquiry, which as a boy I had seen only from an Orthodox Jewish distance, I began in college to find an intellectual home outside the Orthodox Jewish world. Secular learning, with its seemingly limitless reach, was much more appealing than the theologically limited scholarship of the *yeshiva* or ritual study of the synagogue study hall.

I became attracted to the social sciences, to anthropology and sociology. As my religious parents and grandparents had spent hours over holy books, I spent my time reading the classics of social science, trying to discover through them the meaning people gave to their lives and the ways they exhibited their character. Gradually, my Jewish library—the holy books I had been collecting since my *bar mitzva* in hopes that I might someday penetrate them and discover their value for me—became pushed aside by the literature of my new discipline. Where volumes of Judaica had once sat, I now placed books by the giants in my field: Franz Boas, Emile Durkheim, Erving Goffman, Margaret Mead and Max Weber. My shelves still contained holy books like *Ethics of the Fathers* and *The Code of Jewish Law*, the great moral and legal compass of Jewish tradition; but more often than not it was my teacher Erving Goffman's seminal studies *The Presentation of Self in Everyday Life* and *Behavior in Public Places* that I took in hand to study and peruse. While my way of life remained that of Orthodox Judaism, my career became sociology. Both background and career made their claims upon me, and thus I made my way between the particular demands of each. My heart and home were Jewish, but my mind and work became more and more caught up in the thicket of my academic discipline.

Culture embedded in the lives of people all around me, more than ancient sacred texts, was what I devotedly tried to read. The creations of humanity and the rules of social behavior rather than the machinations of God or religious law aroused my interest. The ancient sacred provinces of Judaism—the universe of the Talmud—seemed increasingly distant and limited. They described a world that hardly seemed real. Laws concerning ancient Temple sacrifices, disputations about whose ox gored whom or tales of humble scholars and brilliant rabbis were hardly of concern to a young intellectual—even an Orthodox one. It was sociology and anthropology I wanted and felt an obligation to study, not the venerable holy books of my people.

Quietly, I sometimes attempted to forget about trying to penetrate the world of the Talmud and *lernen*. I sought instead to sing the tune of the times and be in harmony with the contemporary world. The singsong of *Gemara lernen* was dissonant with that aim; it seemed to shift one inescapably into the past. Laboring through Talmud pages or sitting with men who reviewed them endlessly seemed to me a drag on my movement into the present and its surroundings.

But even after college I could not forget about *lernen*. The competing authorities of my social science were insufficient, their vision flawed by an almost obstinate flight from all truths. A capacity to observe all life from some neutral, objective distance and the celebration of cultural relativity, while perhaps useful for scientists, could not replace the Jewish world completely. It did not provide me with a spiritual anchor. One might live *off* sociology and anthropology, but to me it seemed impossible to live *for* them. A person needed more. Besides, I knew that in the natural order of my Jewish life, a man was not complete—was not a man—if he forever abandoned his obligation to *lern*. However modern I might be, I was still attached to that sacred duty. If I did not engage in *lernen* it was not because I summarily rejected its legitimacy. I just did not know how I could make that old way of study fit into my new frame of mind.

As I made my way into the outside world, acquired new perspectives and found myself an occupation, I tried increasingly to keep my Judaism in private regions. Outside I was a modern man, while in the house a secret Jew—a kind of moral Marrano. The situation bothered me until at last I found a way to combine my public and my private faces, to once again make the old new and the new holy.

My training was as a sociologist and anthropologist and my interest had always been in matters Jewish. In my career, I found a way to combine those interests by looking at Jewish life in much the same way that people with my training had in the past studied and explained the native peoples of the Pacific or

Africa. While they had studied Trobriand Islanders or Zulu warriors, I had looked at Orthodox Jews—a people whose contribution to civilization no one could deny. I could wander about in the Orthodox world while playing my role as a social scientist.

In the best traditions of my craft, the approach that I had always used was that of participant-observer, becoming part of what I observed. But there was an important difference: my colleagues were neither Trobriand Islanders nor Zulus, but I was, or at least had been, an Orthodox Jew.

The preferred approach, I had often been told, was to begin as an outsider. Natives got too involved and could not see their own world for what it really was. Besides, being a social anthropologist was something that required an exquisite capacity for professional distance—and how could natives of any sort be expected to accomplish that? But I believed, more and more, that it was easier to teach a native how to distance himself from his own people and way of life and then describe where he had been than it was to make an outsider fully comprehend what it meant to be a native. Natives, with the proper discipline, could be aware of nuances of existence, be sensitive to motivations and moods, could look into their world with a far clearer eye and more fully than could any outsider, however well trained. Besides, I had personal reasons for my stance.

Over time, through observation and the tools of my social-science discipline, I thought I had learned to balance myself between the inside and outside, to distance myself from the world in which I lived so that it might be more objectively observed. There was, of course, a special problem: all the time my colleagues worried about "going native," my constant fear was "going stranger"—becoming too alienated from my own community and environment.

When early in my career I had chosen to investigate and

document my own Orthodox synagogue life, I had done so believing that as an insider I could supply, through both introspection and a sense of the relevant questions to ask, information about dimensions of inner life not readily available to other researchers. I argued in sociology journals and before academic audiences that by doing this I would be able to give a fuller picture of the synagogue than could any outsider, however well prepared and trained he might be.

I did not plan to write about the synagogue out of any religious sensibility—or so I led myself to believe at the outset. I simply chose a setting I knew best, one I could sociologically exploit and expertly describe. But to accomplish this, I spent more time in the synagogue than ever before in my life and in the process discovered more of its meaning for me than I had ever imagined possible at the outset. And when I had finished my book, I realized that the double pattern of my life had repeated itself in my work: I had found my way back into the traditional synagogue from my new home in the university via the tools of my social science. At the same time that I had pursued my vocation, I had been able to bring together the two worlds I inhabited. Participant-observation was, at least in part, for me yet another expression of my modern Orthodoxy.

But *lernen* still remained outside my reach and beyond the capacities of my profession—or so I thought until one Friday night when my rabbi inquired, as usual, about my *lernen*.

I had come to the Friday-evening synagogue service quite early, and no one else except the rabbi was there. As always, he sat over an open book. Seeing me walk in, he called me over to sit beside him as he *lernt* a page of Talmud. The long, thick columns, the boldface letters told a tale he thought I knew.

"It bears *lernen*," he explained, and he proceeded to review the familiar history of Yochanan ben Zakkai. For some reason —perhaps it was the dramatic way the rabbi read the text or the story he recounted—my mind was held at attention that evening as I listened to him and followed his finger down the page.

The narrative over, the rabbi looked up from the text and, with the book still open, began to recount the history of Jewish study. He told me how for some, study became vocation—rabbis, *yeshiva* students, scholars. Others, like me, immersed in other pursuits, injected the review of the sacred texts into the ebb and flow of their lives. Evenings, in the morning after praying, at the Sabbath table, they would by way of *lernen* enter, for a time, the holy regions. The Book became the entrance to the temple, the study of it worship. The rabbis and the sages all agreed: "The study of Torah excels all." No Jew could hope to find salvation except by climbing out of the exile of ignorance and into the redemptive light of *lernen*. Study was no longer the practice just of scholars but was for everyone a lifetime mission.

Said Rabbi Yochanan ben Zakkai: "If you have *lernt* much Torah, do not claim credit for yourself, because you were created for this purpose."

"But the Torah," said the sages, echoing Scripture, "is not in heaven." And they added: "Great is the study of Torah, for it gives to those who do it life in this world and in the world to come."

For the rabbis, Scripture—the written word of God—was just the beginning. The Talmud—the great collection of rabbinic commentary and scholarship, the written repository of the Oral Tradition—was its completion, the source of real wisdom, the Book which had preserved and protected the Jewish people since the destruction of the Holy Temple and the exile that followed.

The move from Scripture to Talmud is an ascent to the higher regions of wisdom. This journey could be made alone by those who had skill and dedication. The rabbis of the Talmud, however, had encouraged study in a group. "The words of the Torah cannot be sustained by the solitary individual," the sages asserted. Members of the *chavruse*—the study circle—could help one another reach the heights. Sitting down together over the long pages and working their way through narrative and debate, they open up a way that leads through tales and conversation to what once was and can still be the heavenly Jerusalem.

"*Nu?*" my rabbi ended, and held my eyes as tightly as he could.

I said nothing.

He took a deep breath. "Look, you told me many times that you're a sociologist whose method is participant-observation—you learn by watching while doing."

I nodded.

"*Nu*, so go do some participant-observation among those who *lern*. Find your way into a *chavruse*. Discover Yavneh and its scholars. Build a new Jerusalem."

For days I thought a lot about his story, about the centrality of Jewish study in Jewish life and about my own work. The rabbi had told me nothing new, but still there'd been something in his tone, his challenge to me to take my discipline and apply it to my Jewish world, that struck a sympathetic chord. Perhaps I could use my discipline to beat a path to *lernen*.

The idea of me, a modern Orthodox Jew and social anthropologist, observing and participating in *lernen*, a way of life at once foreign and familiar, began increasingly to capture my imagination. The dual character of the project was appealing; it fitted neatly into the pattern of my life and work. I'd do again what I had done already in the synagogue. I would enter an experience, identify with those who *lernt*, in hopes that this might finally reveal to me and others what so attracted those who did it but eluded me still. Besides, I felt a lingering Jewish obligation to try once more to reach the Torah's heights. This double motivation upon a dualistic man was just enough to move me forward into *lernen*.

I was due for a sabbatical; I had been seeking a research project to fill that time. Now I had one: to examine at first hand the study of Talmud and the people who engage in it.

I talked about the idea with Ellin, my wife. Like me, she led a double life. While I had gone to college an Orthodox Jew and discovered Western civilization, she had come there from an assimilated American family and found her Judaism. We had met at the crossroads, and there we lived. It was she who bought me my set of the Talmud at the time of the birth of our first child. For years the tall, thick volumes sat on my shelf untouched. Still, a Jewish home needed these holy books, Ellin believed. And our Jewish son deserved a father who studied them.

"Even if that means I spend less time with my family?" I asked her.

"But it's important for you to do. I think you'll be a better father for your children because of it. You'll set the right example."

"Even if I do it primarily as a sociological research project?"

She smiled and quoted me a line from the Talmud that I had used many times to explain why I performed certain ritual observances—what we Jews call *"mitzvos"*—even though I had a hard time believing in their religious significance. "A man should always perform the *mitzvos* even if he does not believe in them, since by doing so he will come to believe."

"Even if this kind of *mitzva* excludes you?" I asked finally. There were no women in the traditional house of study; it was a kind of men's club, where even God seemed always to be male.

"We each have our own *mitzvos* to perform, each in our own way."

For several weeks the project grew and developed in my mind, as I tried to formulate a plan of study. At last, I resolved to go to synagogues and little study halls, the *bes medresh*, where circles of men lingered over holy books. For such men the review of Talmud was not simply a duty to be performed but a pleasure to be embraced; for them the world of the page was ineluctably connected with life. Only by entering into the life of the study circle could I perhaps for once, and maybe never again in my lifetime, share the experience of *lernen* and discover the meaning it held for those who engage in it. But I was not at all sure exactly how to find these people of the Book.

For a time, I wandered into Talmud classes at a number of local synagogues. But as I tried to attend to turns of logic and Talmudic reasoning, I got hopelessly lost and frustrated. I could still not connect what I was hearing with what I already knew. So I focused my attention on matters of language and interaction. The approach was strictly sociological. Yet while this approach allowed me to analyze the way in which the Jews I observed studied their sacred texts, it did not allow me to enter into the experience, to participate fully, to share their states of being. I needed to go elsewhere.

"There are ten portions of wisdom in the world," said the sages, "nine in Jerusalem and one in the rest of the world."

No place seemed better for the effort than where it had all begun so long ago. Besides, I had never been to Israel and thought that as a Jew who sought to enter the heart of a Jewish experience I ought to go to the spiritual center of the Jewish people. Over the centuries, the spirit of Yavneh had found a home in the Holy Land. And so at last we went—my wife and sons and I—up to Jerusalem.

I did not know then that what began as a sabbatical would end as a pilgrimage; that my participant-observation would reach its limits; that I, charmed and transformed by my experience, would have to go beyond my role of sociologist. In the end, and after the experiences I shall here recount, I would write and publish my sociology of *lernen*; I'd find my way back to the university. But before that, the holy books that my social science had made me set aside would at last lay claim on me and I'd be touched in ways I could not at the start have imagined. My training and discipline would help me see a great deal but would finally prove insufficient for me to share fully in all I saw.

All of this would happen very soon. Jerusalem would quickly overcome me; the spirit of Yochanan ben Zakkai would overwhelm Goffman, Mead, Durkheim, Weber and all my sociology. I would enter a gate that took me behind the wall of my resistances and into the columns of Talmud and the world of the men around them. I would be buffeted between the extremes of "going native," of losing myself among those who lived only inside the pages, and of hopeless estrangement, during which I felt awfully alone. In the end I would again—as I had throughout my life—find my way between the two extremes.

On this journey into *lernen* I would discover people for whom Jewish study is more than a matter of scholarly erudition, for whom it is an extension and a fulfilment of deeply felt religious obligation. My guides would be simple people, the sort one hardly notices—alms collectors and book dealers, bank tellers, preachers and mystics. But these people would enable me to realize at last for myself that the Talmud is not simply another book but rather a human translation of God's Oral Law, a monument of religion and culture, a symbol of historical identity for my people—a people for whom the book or scroll, more than the picture or statue, is the preferred emblem of their survival in exile.

I would discover that those who recite and reiterate Talmudic controversies, review and react to the text's logic, use its terminology, perceive the world through its perspectives, reaffirm the legitimacy of its laws and the authenticity of its narratives, and accept the necessity of its theological limitations do more than engage in an intellectual acquisition of knowledge. They at the same time form and discover their temperament and the temper of their people—my people. As I would listen to the *lerners* bring to life the voices in the Talmud—the words were always read aloud, sometimes even chanted—I would come to understand that the students not only learn what the texts have to say; they also have a chance to reenact, enter and bring to life the ageless world of the rabbinic academy and the tradition upon which it stands. Like the speakers on the page open before them, the men I joined engaged in debates, asked questions, told stories or digressed with their fellows along a circuitous and historical path of Jewish associations.

Lernen, a spiritual meditation on and lifelong review of Jewish holy books, I would realize, is an effort to shred time and overcome loneliness, a way of attaching oneself to one's people through the medium of a text, a traditional and direct encounter with the Jewish substance in tradition.

Not until I had been to Jerusalem and observed and joined in the act of *lernen* the Talmud would I be able to discover its centrality to my own Jewish existence. To enter into the process of *lernen* with the people who are embraced by it and share in their experience, I would have to face and go beyond the limits of my objectivity, to overcome my feelings of estrangement from the ritual study of ancient texts, to find a way to reweave the fabric of my life. What had begun by engaging the social scientist in me would end by awakening the Jew.

ONE

There Are Two Clocks in the House of Study

"THE earthly Jerusalem which sits atop Zion," said the ancient Talmudic sage Rabbah in the name of his teacher Rabbi Yochanan, "is not like the heavenly Jerusalem. Into the Jerusalem of this world all who wish to ascend may ascend; but into the heavenly Jerusalem only the invited may ascend and enter."

While only invitations may get one through the gates of the heavenly Jerusalem, a walk along its earthly avenues and alleys allows at least a glimpse of that other reality. For weeks, I wandered through the city to get a feel for what it was. A stream of images washed over me, and even now those visions come back to me with all the freshness of a first impression.

Inside a sleek and streamlined bus that winds its way through the contemporary, western side of the city, a friar in sackcloth robe sits. Amid the sound and rhythm of the modern world, his quiet solitude seems somehow still unbroken. Along a downtown street awash in shoppers and tourists, a hooded, black-draped figure floats silently past: an Armenian monk with headdress shaped like his holy Mount Ararat is on his way back to his monastery. Behind a small and faceless door beside the city's outdoor market, a group of pious Jews with bearded faces and wiry earlocks reviews an ancient sacred text through which they glimpse another place, another time. Their voices rise and fall in special cadences; their dialogue puts life into immemorial words. In a corner of the busy central bus station, as people rush to make their connections, a dark-skinned Yemenite Jew sits and quietly recites the Psalms from a shredded little book he holds in hand, his body slowly swaying back and forth.

A walk or drive toward the east and there, inside it all, surrounded by its modern counterpart, the aged city sits, a vision of that other time and other place. Behind its ancient walls, where those who dwell in higher regions may easily feel at home, are other faces, other rooms. Some anchor one to here and now and some to the hereafter. Through one of seven gates inside its ageless golden walls, left and up neglected stairs, across the alley from the Arab souk filled with eager shoppers and shrewd or enterprising merchants who offer every earthly pleasure, one comes up onto the roof of the Church of the Holy Sepulchre. There, in eerie silence, appears a little village of Ethiopian monks who keep a vigil in this holy place. The one-room adobe huts in which they dwell are closed from view. In a small green wooden door, a tiny window through which the passerby may glance reveals a little cot and a cross upon the wall. And in the courtyard stands a small black man. He leans against a green wrought-iron railing, his arms draped around the banister in what seems a loving embrace. He smiles and lets the visitor inside the tiny chapel he must guard. And there the other time and other place can once again be seen—this time more clearly than before—but still not entered uninvited.

The bells of nearby churches begin to toll, and suddenly cassocks appear; doors open and once again are closed. And

through it all, the muezzin calls and lines of Moslems begin to
form as people make their way five times each day to worship in
the place from which Mohammed ascended into heaven. The
one Jerusalem increasingly intrudes upon the other.

Around another corner is a door, and then an alley. Turn left
and right, then turn once again and climb, and there another
crossroads between the heaven and the earth. Here is a Jerusalem that is more than simply a place on the map. Here is the
embodiment of an idea, a symbol of a glorious past and hopes
for the future. El Aqsa and its silver dome sits atop the mountain from which Mohammed left for heaven, on which the Holy
Temple of the Jews once stood and where, before it all, Abraham bound Isaac and prepared to send him to another place
far different from the one he knew.

The Holy Temple is long gone. Destroyed at first by Baby-
lonians and then rebuilt and burned again, this time by Romans,
who left only the outer walls, half crumbling—against which
now the Jews, returned, still whisper prayers and pause within
their daily lives to get a glimpse of holiness. Between the cracks
are notes with names and quoted lines of Scripture which those
on earth have sent to God in hopes that through this little act of
piety they'll keep the gates of heaven slightly open and let their
spirit rise on through. For those who press their faces against
the ancient stones, the object of their prayers is a passage to the
heavenly Jerusalem whose gates mirror those of the earthly one.

A Jew once steeped in this tradition, I stood for many hours
before this holy place. While staring at the sacred stones and
those who seek an entry into heaven there, I could not but think
of Jews who raise themselves by other means. For them neither
prayers nor acts of special piety at venerable walls lead the way
to higher regions, but rather meditation and review of hallowed
books. That way, as I already knew, had begun with Yochanan
ben Zakkai, who led his people from crumbling holy stones to

sacred books and learning, a path which in some way I stood ready to follow.

Gazing out one morning at the Old City, with its impressive walls and imposing history, I realized that while its temporal gates were easy enough to find, it might be quite a bit harder to discover the gateways to *lernen* and gain entry into a *chavruse*. To follow in the steps of Yochanan ben Zakkai, who had made Torah study the great new edifice of Jewish life, I supposed I had to begin at the Temple Mount and then come away from its relic remains to the living temple which had been created in the world of Jewish study. Where once the sound of sheep going to the slaughter on the Temple Mount must have filled the air, the voices of Jews reviewing their sacred texts could now be heard through the windows of the *yeshivos* and houses of learning that dotted the Jewish Quarter of the city.

To reach that quarter, I walked from where I stood on a hill on the western side of the valley toward the ancient walls on the other side. Those walls were relics of generations past. Buried by centuries of debris, they had been uncovered by the Jews who had gained control over them in 1967. What archeologists had discovered was that each new ruler of the city had built his walls on or near the remains of the previous walls. There one could find two-thousand-year-old Herodian stones mixed in with older Hasmonean blocks and next to Crusader bricks, all of which were used anew by Turks in the sixteenth century. In the ramparts of the Old City of Jerusalem, time had been shredded and history rewoven. Old walls made new through a process of uncovering seemed the right metaphor for my own quest.

I walked through the Jaffa Gate, the busiest and in many ways most imposing entrance, and turned southward, shuffling through the sea of cultures in the square inside. Behind me now were the Arab Christians whose homes spread out around the Via Dolorosa and the Church of the Holy Sepulchre. On the left I would pass the Armenians, who, living within the walls of a monastery which closed its gates at nine each evening, tended to keep very much to themselves. Between these two quarters was an eddy of tourists from the West and Moslems on their way in to the bazaars on David Street which served as a kind of spine down this backside of the city. And just beyond the Armenians and ending at the Western Wall, the last remaining structure of the Holy Temple which once had stood where a golden-domed Mosque now did, was the Jewish Quarter, where I hoped my entrance into the heavenly Jerusalem, the way of *lernen*, could be found.

Like all of the Old City, the Jewish Quarter is a maze of narrow streets and alleys, many of which have names that resonate Scripture, Talmud and Jewish history. Inside, the combination of the foreignness of the surroundings and the familiarity of the names made me at once anxious about continuing and reluctant to turn around and leave. Perhaps it was all those years of repeating in my prayers that Jewish longing for Jerusalem, perhaps simply the lure of the new; maybe it was the sound of Hebrew that echoed from the windows of the quarter and the steady rise-fall cadences of Talmud study that I heard when I passed near the doorway of Yeshivat ha-Kotel. Whatever the source of my attraction, the result was an undeniable desire to move further and further into the heart of this Jewish part of the city.

Crossing a large square near Yeshivat ha-Kotel, the Talmudic academy set up almost in the shadow of the Temple Mount, I found myself walking along a street called simply "Rechov ha-Yehudim"—Street of the Jews. To my right was a small sign that marked the entrance to a "Chabad House," one of the outposts of the Lubavitch Hasidic movement. Lubavitch, with its rebbe, or charismatic leader, Rabbi Menachem Schneerson of Brooklyn, was one of the few groups of Hasidim that enthusiastically greeted Jewish seekers, one of whom—like it or not—I had in a way become. And "ChaBaD" was the acronym for *chachma* (wisdom), *bina* (understanding) and *da'at* (knowledge)—the three great rungs of Jewish study which Lubavitch had taken as its motto. I thought therefore that here was a place where I might find the way in—if not to *lernen* then perhaps to wisdom, understanding or knowledge.

Opening the door, I entered a small courtyard from which led other doors on all four sides. In a corner was a stone staircase leading to the sound of voices engaged in study. But these were the young voices of *yeshiva* boys reviewing their texts—not the sort of circle I was prepared to enter. So rather than ascending the stairs, I went instead toward the left and what appeared to be a rather large office.

It was late morning, and most of the place was empty. There were some pamphlets and holy books lying about, and I picked them up to get an idea of who visited this place. The booklets were in English and French and were filled with what could best be called advertisements for God—pitches pushing the observance of those commandments which the Rebbe had decided were the key to getting Jews back onto the proper religious path. For women there was a little booklet about the importance of lighting the Sabbath candles and for the men one on why and how to don *t'filin*—phylacteries.

The holy books were something else. These were for those who had already been persuaded of the value of a traditional life and wanted to plumb its spiritual depths. Here was a copy of the *Tanya*, a collection of the wisdom of the founder of ChaBaD, filled with homilies, moral teachings and epigrams about Scripture and Jewish mystical texts. And then, of course, there were some volumes of Bible and Talmud.

Hearing footsteps coming toward me, I picked up the *Tanya*. Perhaps I supposed that once seen holding this text—so venerated by the followers of ChaBaD—I would be greeted as one who knew or at least appreciated what Lubavitch had given Judaism, that I would be treated with the warmth afforded an insider. This turned out to be true.

The man who entered glanced at me and then at the book in my hands and gave a nod and a smile. *"Shalom aleichem,"* he said, greeting me in the traditional way. *"Aleichem shalom,"* I answered. He was the overseer, the *gabbai*, of the house. He was all in black; his coat, his black velvet *yarmulke*, his beard and earlocks were relics of a world undreamed of on these streets in the days of Yochanan ben Zakkai. As we chatted in Hebrew, he told me that he was a French Jew who, at the urging of the Rebbe, had emigrated several years earlier from Strasbourg and had been assigned responsibility for the house. We shared the small talk of Jerusalem's Jewish Quarter: what had brought him here, how grand it must be to be housed so close to the Temple Mount, the splendid way the Jewish community had rerooted itself in the land of its forebears, the great merit of studying Torah in the "special atmosphere of the Holy City." So began our encounter.

Now he offered to show me around the house. We walked from room to room around the courtyard until at last we came to a small room just off the nursery where some of the children were being taught the ways of Judaism under the guidance of Hasidism. In this little room, which to me seemed to have all the makings of a shrine, was a scale model of what appeared to be an undistinguished brick tenement, of a sort that is commonly found on the streets of New York. This was no child's toy, for it was housed under glass and had clearly been constructed with meticulous care. Even the fire escapes along the side were perfect duplications.

I had seen many models of the Holy Temple all over Jerusalem—in schools, synagogues, toy stores and even at a hotel. But here, literally in the shadow of the Temple Mount, I found a model of a Brooklyn tenement.

"What's this?"

"It's the Rebbe's *yeshiva,*" my host explained. Here was a replica of the Lubavitch World Headquarters, the apartment building at 770 Eastern Parkway. This, for the faithful in Chabad House, was the new shrine, the new temple.

At first this struck me as a kind of idolatry, an obdurate denial of Jewish history. But then as I stood there, it began to dawn on me that in a way that house in Brooklyn was no different from the Talmudic academy that Yochanan ben Zakkai had begun in Yavneh, when he sought refuge from the then-besieged city of Jerusalem. The Temple was about to be destroyed; the future lay with those who would study Torah. The Temple was *still* destroyed, and for the followers of the Lubavitch Rebbe, it was still the Yavneh of 770 Eastern Parkway that protected the Jews.

Standing there looking at the model, I turned to my guide and said:

"I really came here to find a *chavruse.*"

There was no need to say more, no need for us to launch into a philosophical discussion about the merits and mandates of study. We both knew that that meant I wanted to join a circle of others and regularly review Talmud, not for profit or a vocation but because that was a religious obligation of all Jews. We spoke the same language, lived in a universe of like moral obligations and worshiped the same God. This man whom I had never met before knew me, knew who I was and where I wanted to go. And all this was quietly yet efficiently confirmed when I told him of my hopes for finding a *chavruse.*

It struck me then as it has often on other occasions what a

splendid thing it was to be a Jew who could feel at home within the precincts of tradition. Wherever that sort of Jew went and whatever strangers he met, when each identified the other as a Jew bound by the same religious bonds, both felt as if they were old acquaintances. It helped surmount feelings of anxiety about places and people. It made one feel instantly at home.

Those who had often criticized the Jews as being part of some separate order, "a state within a state," unwilling to be absorbed by the non-Jewish world around them, were correct in their perceptions. Few Jews remained who still fitted this contra-acculturative model. But I could, when I wished, be among them. And today this struck me as particularly fortunate. It was good to feel at home.

"How about joining the boys upstairs?" he asked. I wanted something a little less formal and institutional.

"Well," he went on, "there's a place in Shaarey Chesed where there are always some men sitting and *lernen*." Shaarey Chesed —literally, "gates of kindness"—was a section of town that lay between the market district and the high-class neighborhoods of Rehavia. Here in one of the interstices of this special city, I would find a group of people for whom Jewish study was as much a part of their lives as eating and sleeping—and sometimes indistinguishable from them. Many of the men were old, I was warned, but they would readily accept me into their circle, for to them the study of Torah was a haven into which all Jews had to be welcomed, whether old or young. Better the old who are at home with their *lernen* than the young who are obsessed by it, I thought.

The next day I found my way to Shaarey Chesed and to the large synagogue there. It was late afternoon, the time of the *mincha* prayers, and soon the light inside would be brighter than that on the outside. It was the time when men are on their way home from work and stop into the *shul* much as their counter-

parts elsewhere might stop into the pub, to share some time with
their friends in an atmosphere of cultural intimacy and warmth.
Downstairs from the main sanctuary were four or five rooms
which made up the *shul* and the *bes medresh*, the house of
prayer and study that served the day-to-day needs of the worshipers. These were simple rooms, with a small vestibule in
which were some shelves filled with *shamos*—the remnants of
holy books too worn and torn to be used any longer but which
still needed to be stored. And in front of these shelves were two
long tables on which lay a variety of books not yet worn
enough to be *shamos* but no longer sturdy enough for constant
use. The rooms themselves were marked by long wooden tables
and matching benches, smoothed by generations of men who
had sat, worshiped and studied at them. At the front of each
room, facing toward the Old City, was a small Ark, made of
carved olivewood and beechwood. All the other walls were
covered with memorial tablets and inscriptions. There were
lamps burning everywhere, and fluorescent lights around whose
circle could be seen little black letters memorializing a former
rabbi. There were doorposts commemorating a lost child or
bookcases named after a departed teacher. Indeed, it seemed
that every light bulb and shelf had been consecrated in someone's memory. And everywhere there were books. They were of
all sizes; the large tomes of the Talmud sat near little psalters or
worn prayer books. There were commentaries on the *Mishna*
and Maimonidean presentations of the law or guides for the
perplexed.

Like the men around me, I walked in for *mincha*. And when
I did so, I entered another world. The faces were different from
those seen on the street outside. In place of the blank look that
marked the faces of most passersby, the men I now saw had eyes
that reflected the pages in front of them. They appeared transformed into scholars at study. The laborer in his dingy jacket,

the pensioner with a face made tired by time, the shopkeeper all blended into the environment inside. Even those who sat in small klatches and quietly chatted seemed now as if engaged in the most erudite discussions of Talmud. Their furrowed brows, the thumbs digging imaginary ditches in the air as their voices rose and fell in the Yiddish cadences of debate and controversy, the swaying of men huddled together and over old books made me realize that in here all the identities and interests which absorbed those men outside were submerged in a sea of Talmudic logic and digression.

The transformation began in the little hall one entered when coming in from the street. Here was a kind of bridge over which one passed to or from the world outside. Men came in and placed a kiss on the *mezuza* on the door with their right hand while with their left they might grab a prayer book or one of the other texts on the tables. Some simply slid their hands along the tabletop, as if the mere feel of the study table could magically change them from simple men into those who were at home in the *bes medresh*.

Here could be found the overflow from the rooms on either side. One or two men wandered through the knots of people, collecting money or jotting down what for a time seemed to me to be cryptic notations which I later would learn were pledges of charity for one or another community need. Others sat huddled in conversation or lost in reverie.

I passed between the men who stood along the walls and turned into the room on the right, into the *bes medresh* proper. The hum that I had heard from outside became a roar. Everywhere men sat and spoke, either to one another or to themselves; and everyone sat with a book open before him.

When I was a boy we often received calendars around the time of Rosh ha-Shanah from Jewish old-age homes in America and Israel. On these there were often pictures or photos of pious-

looking old men, with long beards and wearing hats or black
velvet *yarmulkes* whose faces had for me always been associated
with the true face of faith. They were always pictured sitting
around tables and poring over the old holy books. In my youth-
ful fantasies, these old men were among the thirty-six righteous
men who legend has it secretly save the world through their
acts of devotion and piety. Although worlds away from Boston
and the lines of my life there, these little old men seemed part of
the Jewish universe I also inhabited. Still, they were always
physically elsewhere, in my consciousness but never in my
presence. Now, suddenly and overwhelmingly, I had stepped
into the photograph and found myself among them.

I sat down in an open spot at one of the tables. The aroma of
perfumed snuff was everywhere, mixed with the pungent odor of
rotting leather, a smell I associated with the bindings of old
books and old *t'filin*, both of which were to be found in
abundance here.

"*Siman lamed ches, din mem heh, ha-chayavim be t'filin ve
hapeturim*"—Chapter Thirty-eight, the laws of who is required
to don phylacteries and who is not. The man next to me handed
me a volume of the Mishna Brura, the codex of Jewish law, and
bade me open to the proper page. And with that I was pulled
into this circle in which I would dwell for more than a year.

I held my eyes to the page, but whenever we engaged in some
brief discussion of and digression from the text, I stole a look
around me. The room was small, like all the others on the
ground floor of this synagogue. It served as one of the many
chambers in which men would recite their daily prayers morning, afternoon and evening. But in between their prayers, they
would use this space and the others like it—sitting around the
tables that lined the walls or leaning against the *shtenders*, or
lecterns, on which they had placed their holy books in the style
of the *yeshiva* student—for *lernen*. Everyone I looked at

seemed immersed in the content of the page in front of him. With their fingers on the place or an arm resting on the large volumes, they seemed at times to lean bodily into what they were reading. And what reading there was! This was not the silent perusal that I might see in my university library. Instead, the men around chanted their texts in the singsong of *gemore-nign*, the unbroken melodic line that infected and inflected Yiddish but had its origins somewhere further back in a legendary Jewish primordial past. *Gemore-nign* was the heart-cry that was mediated by the language and logic of Jewish learning in the world of Eastern Europe. As I watched those around me, it seemed as if they took in the page with their eyes, touched it with their fingers, moved it through their consciousness and echoed it in their voices. Into and out of them it came, and then it filled the room and entered them again.

In time, I would learn how to tune in to various of the sounds of *lernen* I heard around me. And then sometimes, I would pull away and tune in elsewhere. It was like turning the radio dial— except that here instead of moving from music to news and then to a talk show, I could retune from the study of Talmud to a review of codes or else to a discussion of *midrash* and legend.

Time here seemed transformed as well. It was not just that I had left the Jerusalem of the nineteen eighties outside and entered what appeared to be the world of prewar Eastern Europe, but more. Even the specific time inside seemed different. On the wall across from me were two clocks resting on a handsomely carved shelf. These were old pendulum clocks, with Roman numerals on their faces. But one had the time set according to the watch on my wrist and a second, identical in every respect, was set at twelve. Even their pendulums seemed set to go in opposite directions, with one swinging to the right just as the other swung to the left. Later I learned that the left clock was always set to the time in the outside world while the other was set to correspond with the ever-changing time of sunset according to which prayer and study were to be coordinated. The left clock was used to tell men when they had to get to work or had to leave for home; the other told them when they could linger in the pages of a prayer book or the folios of the Talmud. In here one remained aware of the time on the left clock, but one lived in the time on the other.

This was the best time to find men in the *bes medresh*: the twilight hour, between the afternoon *mincha* and the *ma'ariv* prayers of the evening. It had long been a tradition to spend this hour engaged in study. "Meditate upon the Torah day and night," God commanded Joshua upon the entry of Israel into the Promised Land. Well, if so, what better time to review the sacred texts than a time that is both day and night? And so the men who spent their time at work and only their afterhours engaged in study of the Torah more often than not stopped in for *mincha* on their way home from work and spent the time waiting to complete the prayers of the day *lernen*.

At first, everyone around me seemed a part of a sea of pious-looking faces. There were those with long beards and earlocks whose faces reflected a pious past and others who, while appearing a bit more contemporary in their grooming and dress, still exuded a quiet piety. A black hat, a tightly held holy book, a knitted *yarmulke*—all these marked the others as being at home in the *bes medresh*. In time, however, I would be able to see the lines of cleavage that crisscrossed the room; I would discover the differences between those who gathered in one room and in another, between those poring over texts on a table in the corner and those leaning into books around *shtenders*, between those who sojourned in the precincts of tradition and those who dwelt there. But for now they were all one people of the Book.

Around the table with me were five other men. One, who sat

in the middle, acted as teacher and read aloud from the text
open before all of us. His was the most striking of faces. Rosy-
cheeked and ringed with long white hair and a silky white beard
which seemed to come to a point just below his collarbone, it
seemed too perfect the image of a sage to be real. On his head
he wore a big, wide-brimmed black hat that was perfectly
rounded on top. Made of felt but heavily smudged with soot, it
was different from the velvet *biber* (beaver) hats that so many
of the others wore, for it seemed to carry no pretensions of
lingering majesty. It was a simple hat of a simple man. And
unlike so many of the others who wore black coats, his was a
gray gaberdine which hung loosely on his small and narrow
frame. Its huge pockets were filled with little notebooks tied
together by a variety of rubber bands and strings: books in
which, I later learned, he kept a variety of records. In one book
he kept a list of funds he collected for the "dowries of poor
brides." In another was a list of subscribers and patrons whose
donations would be used to publish his *sefer*, a holy book filled
with Talmudic and other Jewish epigrams. I would hear some of
them in the months ahead: "Better an ugly face than a mean
heart"; "Neither with curses nor with derision can one trans-
form another"; "A truly great man is like a tree—we realize his
stature only when he is cut down." It would be a "significant"
contribution to the wisdom of contemporary literature, he once
assured me as he added my name to his unending list.

Next to the teacher sat his friend Reb Tuvia. Reb Tuvia was
nothing of a Hasid. Dressed in a simple jacket and Stetson, he
was one of those fellow-travelers who find comfort among those
who appear more pious. He wore a plastic patch on one of the
lenses of his heavy glasses and seemed always to be suffering
from cold sores. As he sat listening to the teacher, he would tilt
his head so as to turn his better ear and good eye toward the
teacher. It was as if he could thereby overcome the constraints

of his body and sneak his soul through to the world of *lernen*.
He was the most loyal of followers of the text, always attentive
and never absent from a single meeting.

On the teacher's other side, but leaning away from him, was
Moishe. A relatively young man—perhaps in his forties—he
had a look in his eyes that made him appear to be just short of
mad. There was, to be sure, nothing especially lunatic about
him, except perhaps the fact that he seemed to carry on very
short conversations with himself during the *lernen*. But this sort
of behavior was not notably unusual, for the style of study so at
home in this place often required people to appear to be "talking to themselves." What they were really doing was engaging in
dialogue with the texts, reading commentaries aloud and then
responding to them. Most of those who carried on such conversations, however, did so when they studied alone. Moishe did
it within the group. Still, even this was not altogether suspect,
since he might, as others often did, simply be providing a sort
of running commentary or even an echo to the wisdom of the
teacher.

So it was not his talking that made me wonder about Moishe's
sanity. It was, instead, his eyes. They burned. Wide open and
sometimes freezing into an expression of sheer joy, they seemed
to hint that while he appeared to be absorbed in the text, Moishe
was seeing something else beyond it that was driving his emo-
tions and focusing his vision.

Besides these three there were two other men, quiet and in
most respects unremarkable, who sat on my side of the table.
They were bodies who filled the space and took in the Torah. I
cannot say how much they took in, for they seldom uttered even
an echo of anything the teacher spoke. Still, Yaakov and Zeesel,
as these two were called, always joined our circle whenever they
came to *mincha* and stayed until *ma'ariv*.

"Do you understand Yiddish?" the teacher asked me, jarring me out of my reverie of observation on this my first visit.

I was stunned. Certain that I had become all but invisible among all these books and people, I had let my attention wander from the text. Now it was obvious that my presence was not only noticed but about to be acknowledged.

"We can continue in Hebrew, if you like," he added even before I had a chance to reply. And then, as I opened my mouth to answer that I could understand Yiddish but spoke Hebrew better, I heard the thump of a hand from the front of the room.

My teacher smiled and looked down at the small piece of paper he held in his hand. I noticed some numbers written on it. Later I would learn that they were the precise time of nightfall, a time that would change by a minute or two each day. It was this time that had now arrived, and the clap of the hand I had just heard was the *gabbai* reminding everyone that the *lernen* would have to stop for a while during the forthcoming *ma'ariv* prayers.

But this would not be like any *ma'ariv* at which I had ever been present before. To begin with, the pause in the *lernen* did not lead everyone in the room to prayer. Some of those present walked out the door and into another of the chambers, while others streamed in through the door from other rooms or from outside the building. Each time I thought the flow of entering men was over, another would come through the door. Many of those entering were greeted with the traditional Jewish display of respect for scholars. As they passed near, those men who considered themselves lesser in status stood up. But so many of those who moved to stand were themselves wizened by time that it was all they could do just to lean forward and slightly rise from their seats. This made for the curious sight of people popping up and down again and again. It was almost as if I were watching them literally settle down for prayer, something they did physically as well as spiritually.

It would be a while before I knew who stood in honor of whom and why. But even before I was sure of the identities of all these characters, I began my own rises and falls. It simply felt wrong to be settled down completely while others around me continued their standing and sitting.

Everywhere I sensed activity. Here and there one of the money collectors tried to complete one more transaction before everything stopped for prayer. Then too, there were men reciting *Kaddish*, the memorial prayer which often marks the end of ritual study. Others were ending their conversations, replacing books on shelves, displaying respect for their betters and positioning themselves in their favorite prayer nooks in one or another of the room's corners. But in the heart of all this apparently chaotic activity there was a rhythm which seemed to tie it all together, a beat that had begun with the thump of the *gabbai* and that would end with the opening words of the *ma'ariv*: "Bless the Lord, Who is blessed."

When it seemed that everyone was ready to pray, one last man would usually wander in. In his late sixties, shaped a bit like a down-filled pillow and wearing a beard that was streaked with gray, he walked languorously toward the front of the room and sat down along the eastern wall, the place reserved for the most honored among the worshipers. To the uninformed he might have seemed to be wearing a bathrobe and slippers. I had, however, long ago learned that this was the garb worn by the well-dressed traditional Jewish scholar. His "robe" was a brocaded gray caftan, or *kapote*, which indicated a certain noble character. His slippers were the shoes only a scholar who did not spend his day at manual labor or in the world outside the *bes medresh* could wear. As he passed through the room, others stood or leaned forward, and when he reached his place, I saw the *gabbai* nod a signal to the man who would lead us in prayer to commence. And now everyone stood to bow—this time to the holy Ark and not to any mortal—as the *ma'ariv* began.

Later, I would learn that this man for whom we had apparently been waiting was "the Maggid," known throughout Jerusalem as one of the last who still kept up the tradition of true preaching. On Sabbath afternoons he would hold court in this same room, which was then filled to the walls, and would review the portion of the week, weaving into it a variety of homilies and visions, stories and parables. He could, for example, make the Biblical Joseph into a contemporary of everyone in the room and then just as easily sweep all of us gathered around him back into time and into a narrative that dripped with memories of a Jewish world which seemed to have perished in the fires of Nazi Europe. It did not matter whether or not one had actually seen that world for himself, for under the spell of the Maggid one could see it with all the nostalgia of personal reminiscence.

He was a master storyteller, an actor who animated his stories with heart-cries of "Oy-yoy" that could make even the most hardened cosmopolitan into a parochial who yearned for the world of the *bes medresh* and a past that was part of the traditional Jewish consciousness he thought he had long ago abandoned.

The Maggid sat somewhere between his audience and his own imagination. Sometimes I could notice one eye closed and the other carefully watching for the reactions of those who waited on his every word. But this performance was not simply some cynical effort to dazzle those around him. It seemed, rather, a display of the division in the Maggid's being. On the one side—the one on which his eye was open—he was attached to the people he could see before him, trying to satisfy their craving for a spiritual and Jewish experience. But on the other —the side of his closed eye—he looked inward and from thence upward to heaven. Only here he seemed to find the source for what the outer world brought forth from his mouth. It was a complicated business, and often it set him to swaying back and forth or nodding his head up and down, as if he were being simultaneously buffeted and pulled by the concerns of this world and the other.

He did not just tell his stories: he literally sang them. Sometimes he would stop at some particular word that charmed him and repeat it in a variety of voices and melodies until everyone seemed as lost in and fascinated by it as he. It was always a masterly performance, and often I would walk out not quite sure precisely what he had said—but all the same deeply impressed by having heard him say it. In this I was clearly not alone.

"How beautifully he speaks," I once heard someone say. Clearly a part of this experience was aesthetic as much as anything else. Perhaps this was what was meant when people referred to him as a *"shayner Yid"*—a beautiful Jew.

Now, however, as I stood in the small synagogue surrounded by weekday worshipers, I did not yet know about the Sabbath talks. Instead, I simply paid attention to what would happen next.

For a short while, everything seemed to proceed normally. The prayers were swiftly paced, as weekday services commonly are. But then we reached the *Kriyat Shma*, the recitation of the credo of faith which is perhaps the central article of Jewish prayer. It is composed of verses which appear throughout the Bible, and it is known by its electrifying opening line: "Hear O Israel, the Lord our God, the Lord is One." Recited originally, according to tradition, by Jacob's sons as they stood at his deathbed and promised him that they would follow in the faith of their father and his forebears Isaac and Abraham, it has become the single most memorable verse in the liturgy.

For this generation, it has perhaps additional resonances

which emerge from a more recent deathbed. Millions died with these words on their lips as they stood before the Nazi killers who sought to silence once and for all their cry and credo. Many of the men of Shaarey Chesed were survivors of the Nazi onslaught; others were their children and kin. When they intoned these ageless words, in the same accents and cadences as the generations before them, they overwhelmed time and brought back memories that all of us in the room—no matter our age or origin—shared.

Now, the custom of extending the intonation of this line is a long one. As one begins the words "Shma Yisrael," one lifts a hand toward the eyes, which are covered, and calls aloud for all to hear that the Lord is one. One's own voice necessarily becomes caught up in that of others, and the call of those sitting nearby extends it.

I was used to this sort of devotional contagion. What I was unprepared for, however, was the intensity of the call that I heard tonight. Long minutes passed as each word of the Shma was cried out. And between each word—no, each syllable—and the next, there was a pause, as if the worshipers needed to rest and breathe and consider the philosophical possibilities of continuing.

Last among the voices I heard from behind my hand was a very deep one, a bass so profound it seemed less a product of the larynx than an echo of a sound deep within the chest cavity. It was the voice of the Maggid. When he paused, there was silence for a moment—as if everyone had to swallow hard before continuing; and then the congregation resumed the hum and murmur of their prayers as they completed the three paragraphs of the liturgy.

The prayer which normally lasts less than five minutes stretched out for closer to ten. Each man seemed intent on extending his time in the Shma beyond that of his neighbor, as if each were vying with the other for the attention of heaven. The sociologist in me suggested that the displays were for the benefit of partners in prayer, efforts to demonstrate a holier-than-thou commitment to liturgy. But the Jew in me wondered if perhaps these men were not in some way trying to shake their God into attentiveness. It was, after all, the slowest worshiper who could hold on to his Lord the longest.

I cannot say exactly which of these motives moved me. I do know that it was not long before I began to lose myself in prayer and recited these familiar words of the *Shma* with an attachment that I had not had since those days in grammar school when the first conscious motives of prayer invaded my adolescence. These feelings were now, however, more absorbing, for they arose, it seemed, out of the more secure consciousness of maturity. That I could still be so moved by old prayers was a surprise to me. To be sure, I had always told people that that was why I prayed. But now what had been simply a logical argument became a psychological reality. And the convergence of the two was startling and even unsettling.

Tonight, however, on my first night at Shaarey Chesed, my prayers were not yet ready for enthusiastic extension, and so I finished with plenty of time to spare. I looked around and listened to others. In the rush of my own prayers, it was something I did not often have a chance to do.

"*Hishomru lochem . . .*" Beware lest your heart be deceived, and then you turn and serve other gods and worship them; for then the Lord's anger will blaze against you, and he will shut up the skies so that there will be no rain. . . . These lines of prayer, at once familiar to me and yet somehow strange, seemed tonight to resonate with an authenticity I was not used to hearing. The men who spoke them inhabited a land that depended on rain, the land promised and described in what they recited. They could know when their prayers were or were not acceptable simply by looking out the window. Some did just that as they intoned that line.

But it was a different authenticity that struck me that night, for most of those I watched did not look for the rain or any other sort of instant, divine quid pro quo. Instead, they seemed to dwell upon and within their prayers as if the very act of praying were sufficient fulfillment, even more important to them than any anticipated godly response.

It occurred to me then, as never before, that some people prayed not so much to their God as for themselves—for the transformative power of prayer itself. My own expectations of prayer seemed to have been caught at a very different stage. I still looked upon liturgy as a vehicle for requests from some divine Parent. And when I no longer believed that such requests were efficacious or even conceivable, I had ceased praying with devotion and continued mostly out of inertia and the hope that someday my prayers would once again become meaningful to me. But because I believed that forsaking the demands of tradition was far more dangerous than holding on to them— even if that meant that I carried out practices which were often opaque or even devoid of meaning for me—I had kept on praying.

Now, it is customary for the person leading the prayers to wait before reciting the closing words "I am the Lord your God, true and certain" until the most honored man in the congregation has finished his own recitation of the prayer. I wondered here, where there seemed so many rabbis to choose from, who that would be. Many of those I watched seemed likely candidates. As if to tacitly announce their expectation that they could govern the proceedings, many of them deliberately raised their voices and slowed their pace as they approached the closing words. But as each one came to the word *"emes"* (true and certain), his signal was greeted with silence from the cantor, the man who led the service. Gradually the field narrowed to two men who sat against the eastern wall, separated only by the holy Ark which, containing the Torah scrolls, stood in the center.

The man on the right faced slightly toward the windows. His body was thin, his short and clipped beard completely white. To the uninitiated he might have appeared as simply another of those countless men in Jerusalem who wear black coats and black hats. In this room, however, he was a man to be waited for—or at least, so it now seemed. His voice could not be heard, but from the silent movement of his lips and swaying of his body, it was clear that he was still immersed in his prayers. It seemed an unselfconscious display. He might have known that there were many eyes upon him, but he managed to make it appear that his attention was elsewhere. It seemed almost as if he were trying to disappear into his coat. As if he became thinner and thinner. And indeed, he had a curious way of shrugging his shoulders as he swayed so that the coat seemed to rise as if on its own to permit him to tremble with piety inside it.

The other contender—the Maggid—was exactly his antithesis. His basso profundo seemed to shake the walls; his rotund frame seemed about to burst out of his gray brocaded coat. Where the man on the one side seemed to disappear into his prayers, the one on the other seemed to allow the prayers to disappear into him. These were *his* words, it seemed. He had invented them, and now, with each new intonation, it sounded as if he had just thought of what to say. I listened to him and imagined that he was composing the words as he recited them, so that although slowly spoken they had all the freshness of a new insight into the majesty of prayer.

In this race to be last, each man seemed to be playing it his own way. Yet each seemed authentically to be on the track as it had been laid down. As I observed one, I was sure that he deserved to be waited for. But then I looked to the other and knew that he was the one. And while neither seemed conscious of the other, there was no doubt in my mind that neither could have gone on without the other. I cannot say exactly how I knew that then. I do know, however, that in that place and time there could be no mistaking this.

Finally we reached the *Amida*, the silent prayer that is the climax of all Jewish liturgy. Each man stood with feet together, unmoving, and recited the nineteen blessings that make up this devotion. And then the men who stood in this room seemed at once indistinguishable one from another, for all were one with the house of prayer and with one another, seeming to me like a single standing mass. Then slowly, one by one, the murmured prayers ceased, and finally one solitary voice remained: the Maggid's. Then it too fell silent. And I shuddered; for at the moment when that prayer stopped, the spell was broken. A few men closed their books; a few began to chat with one another. Those whose faces had been moved in prayer became once again simple men. Although they still stood inside this little chapel, their faces once again had the profane and distracted look of men outside. And that subtle but unmistakable shift raised my involuntary shudder.

In a moment, the final *Kaddish* was recited and the men began to leave the room. A few stopped next to the Maggid and chatted. His erstwhile competitor, the self-effacing thin man, walked slowly to the bookcase and removed one of the largest books, opened it, seemed to read a brief passage and then replaced it on the shelf. Then he too quietly left the room.

I waited a few minutes, wondering if the room was ever completely abandoned. Now I noticed that the focus shifted from the pulpit in front toward a corner in the rear where a few of the men were moving some of the tables together to form an "L" shape. At the same time, a cherubic-looking little fat man walked toward these tables. I had not noticed him during the prayers, but now, as all those remaining greeted him, it became clear that if the Maggid and his congregation had been the heroes of the *ma'ariv* story, then this man, Rabbi Moses—as I later learned he was called—would be the center of a new drama that was about to begin in this room.

The *gabbai* also joined the group in the corner. Taking a moment to turn off all the lights in the room except for the two that illumined the corner, he next stepped to the bookcase in the back and took out seven volumes of the Talmudic tractate *Zevachim*. This was a text that dealt with the sacrifices which centuries earlier were brought by all believers who came to worship at the Holy Temple.

"Is there a *chavruse* here?" I asked him, although the answer was obvious.

"For the last sixty years, without exception," he answered. For that long had a group been gathering around these tables after the conclusion of *ma'ariv* to review the Talmud. No one of those present had been in the circle all that time, but each one could be linked to another who in turn was linked to someone else who ultimately was tied to one of the originators. Here was the great Jewish chain of being that begins with Moses at Sinai and runs through Joshua, the Elders, the Men of the Great Assembly and generations of others, finally reaching the countless little circles of Jews who continue to review a Torah they believe was once divinely revealed.

"May I join?"

"Please"—and with that I was motioned to sit next to the Rav, who asked me whence I came.

"I now live in Jerusalem," I answered, a bit too literal with the truth. "And I was told by someone in the Old City that here in Shaarey Chesed I would find a *chavruse* that would be glad to let me join and which was steady in its progress through the SHaS."

"Yah, this is true," replied the man I would later come to know as Reb Zanvil.

"So open to page twenty-four, folio B," Reb Asher said.

The men who sat around this table were of my grandfather's generation. It was not simply that they were older; it was that they luxuriated in the past—not just their own but the Jewish people's. In order to join them, I would have to move backward with them.

First came Reb Asher, a man with a gray goatee and big black hat that was something between a homburg and the *biber* hat that most pious Jerusalemites wore. For the seven months that I stayed in this *chavruse*, Reb Asher never once directly acknowledged my presence; but I knew that he was aware of me, for he would answer my questions even as he addressed his remarks to the Rav. Reb Asher was one of those people who seem to take in the world obliquely, who master reality at the fringe of their consciousness. I was never quite sure he was completely present in or aware of his circumstances—but every so often when I was certain that he was dozing or lost in a senile reverie, he would make some piercing remark that swept away any doubts I had about his alertness.

Reb Tzvi was something quite different. He was the great audience to whom everyone wanted to play. He alone knew how to appreciate a good question or a sharp answer—the blood and tissue of *lernen*. The gleam in his eye whenever the Rav produced some flash of insight was what made the rest of us realize that a "good word" had just been offered. His laughter confirmed that a joke was funny; his comprehension completed our consideration of a topic.

It was Reb Tzvi who handed out the snuff at the start of each session. He would remove the large tin from his pocket, tap it carefully with the middle finger of his left hand while he held on tightly with the right so that the powder inside settled and didn't spill when the box was opened. Then, passing the sweet-smelling stuff first to the Rav, he saw to it that everyone else got a pinch between his fingertips, releasing a scent that mingled with the aroma of the dusty room and the yellowing pages of the open books.

Tzvi was always the one who recited the *Kaddish* prayer at the end of the class hour. This alone marked the formal end of our gathering, and he took obvious pleasure in this symbolic gatekeeper's role. It might be the *gabbai* who turned off the lights, but it was Reb Tzvi who turned off our attention. His bushy mustache covered his mouth completely and so I could never be quite sure of his expression, but it often seemed to me that behind that mustache there was a smile which liked to play across his face unnoticed.

Reb Lippe was someone altogether different. While everyone else spoke Yiddish, Lippe spoke in German, for that was what he knew best. An old man who was not part of the Eastern European cultural milieu from which the others had sprung, he was nonetheless now bound together with them through the ties of this *chavruse*. Lippe distinguished himself by his unabashed assertion of Talmudic expertise. He listened to Rav Moses and the others who claimed to know the text well—but it always seemed that he believed that only he truly understood what the page was all about.

This confidence was—it seemed—a comfortable fantasy. Whenever Lippe raised what he was convinced was a truly critical question or offered a sharp responsum, it was systematically dismissed as either fallacious or wrongheaded. But the smile with which he began his remarks remained forever frozen on his face, as if to say that this small contradiction was of no consequence for those such as he was—undiscovered but genuine scholars.

Reb Zanvil made no such claims for himself. He simply settled himself comfortably on the bench next to me and nodded off to sleep. His was not a deep sleep during which he lost full consciousness of where he was; it was instead one of those little naps that one takes in the sure confidence that nothing much will change in the world while one is away. His were daydreams carried on with closed eyes.

To be sure, I was never really certain when Zanvil was asleep or awake, for he had found a way to wedge himself between me, Reb Eliezer on his right and the table and wall so that he could not fall over. Moreover, from the way he held his head it was impossible to tell whether he was simply looking down into the Talmud or had in fact fallen asleep. His fingers slipped along the page almost automatically, and only the most attentive eye could tell when he was there and when he was out. It did not really matter; Zanvil belonged in the circle just as he was. He was a presence even more than he was a voice.

Excluding me, Reb Eliezer was the youngest of the group. Later that year, he would grow a beard and appear to join the ranks of the wizened. But on this first night and for many thereafter, he looked like a relatively young man who had somehow gotten attached to this *chavruse*. I realized later that all the men had once come aboard that way, for that was precisely how the circle extended its life—taking a young man and aging him through the process of *lernen*. A year after I had left this circle, I returned once for a visit and found that Eliezer had moved firmly into the senior ranks and was by then *gabbai*.

Tonight the *gabbai* was still Reb Eliahu. A thin man with an equally thin beard that ringed his face, he wore a small fedora with barely a trace of a brim, unlike any of the other hats seen in Shaarey Chesed. He was dark-complexioned, but still light enough to not be mistaken for a Jew whose forebears came from the Middle East. Eliahu was without doubt a child of Ashkenazic Jewry, a European product and immigrant from the *yeshivas* of Vilna and Volozhin. He rarely smiled, yet the serious demeanor which at first put me off was, I soon discovered, only veneer. Underneath was the same cherub that our teacher Rav Moses was on the outside. In a way, each man was like the other. Eliahu was that thin man with a serious expression who hid inside the chuckling and chubby Moses, and vice versa.

Only Eliahu could challenge Moses successfully, but he rarely did. And only he could stand in for the teacher on those rare occasions when the latter was absent. It was nothing formally established, but it was at the same time something firmly understood. Reb Eliahu had a presence that only the presence of the Rav could limit.

All this left only Reb Yechiel Michl. He was no ordinary student, for each day before joining this circle he would lead a similar study group in the room across the hall. There he enjoyed all the honor and respect that here was accorded to Rav Moses. But while he might be a Rav elsewhere, in this room and at this hour he was simply another of those who *lernt*. This shift of role through which he passed each evening cannot have been altogether easy for him. Indeed, he never really fully accomplished it, for each day he would cue and echo almost every sentence the Rav read or spoke. It was as if he carried on his own class which was nearly synchronous with ours but never identical. When someone asked Rav Moses a question, Reb Yechiel Michl was ready with an answer. And once when a controversy arose between the *gabbai* and the Rav, it was Yechiel Michl who found the solution.

I am not sure how I found a way to fit in among these men. They were so different from me, and yet in a very short time I felt that my presence in the circle was a part of the taken-for-granted order of things.

The nature of what we *lernt* was such that it denied continuing contact with the world outside the room as we knew it.

Talking and reading about sacrifices no longer brought to a Holy Temple no longer standing was by no means easy for me at first; I had always been rather bored by those sections of the Bible in the book of Leviticus which described the order and detail of the priestly activities and sacrifice; so even had I been able to follow every nuance of the Yiddish with which my *chavruse* reviewed these matters, I would have been hard put to get it all straight. But for these men, all that was no problem. They threw themselves into the text and through it back into time. As we sat there in this little ground-floor chapel in Shaarey Chesed, we looked out not on the streets as they now were but on a world of a distant past now magically made present. It took a while for me to find my way around the Temple Mount through the medium of this class, but in time I learned exactly where I could and could not go.

I had to learn exactly what sacrifices could and could not be brought, who would have to bring them and precisely how they were to be handled. But all this was not to be a part of some lessons to be intellectually assimilated. Rather, the learning I did came in through the imagination. All this became apparent to me one evening as I sat down to review *Zevachim* with my *chavruse*.

It was a December evening. The last few days had gone through the Jerusalem weather pattern to which I was fast becoming accustomed. First came the wind carrying with it all the dust from the Judean desert in the east. Next came the rain which washed all the dirt out of the air and spread it as a light layer of mud over everything and everybody. Then came a clear day in which the dampness of winter fairly clung to the cold. There was no place in the city to really warm up, since no one kept the heat on for more than a few hours each day—it was simply too expensive. So while the temperature rarely dropped below forty degrees Fahrenheit, it always seemed colder than a

New England winter, since that forty degrees remained clattering around in one's body forever.

Sitting at the table in Shaarey Chesed, I could still feel the rain, wind and cold of the last few days. It made me glad that Zanvil was wedged against me on the right and the Rav on my left.

Once we entered the world of the Talmud, however, it was rather easy to forget the cold and the present and become warmly wrapped in the heat of Talmudic disputation. In the liminality of the beginning, however, I found myself gone from the present but not yet having arrived at the past. I waited for a cue, an opening.

"Ehhh," the Rav intoned. It was one of those elongated oral pauses which allowed him to get his bearings in a complicated page. It helped us too, especially when the Rav's pace exceeded my own capacity to keep up. The discussion in the Talmud was about exactly how large the Sacrifice of Thanksgiving had to be, and what happened if that offering turned out to be blemished.

I really didn't care. I had never cared about such things, for to me they were archaic beyond imagining. But these men did care. As we reviewed each move the ancient priests would make in their ritual preparation of the sacrifices, I could begin to see all that rush of activity a bit more clearly. It was evident my partners around the table were walking into the page and onto the Temple Mount with all the assurance of old hands. When they came to a discussion of the sprinkling of blood on the altar and wondered aloud whether or not the priest bent his wrist in that act, it took only a quick look back into their own memory to see precisely how the ritual was carried out.

But this memory was of course not theirs in origin; it was a memory acquired from the text. Their many years of review had allowed them to construct that ancient Temple and altar in their minds and people it with priests and worshipers. It only seemed to me—the outsider—that they were looking into their own memories.

When I had first come upon these men, I had seen them as hopelessly archaic, charming throwbacks to another age. Sitting now with them and watching them spiritedly chart their way into a past which I, as a Jew, shared with them, I began to look at myself as hopelessly trapped in my own time. And so even though I cared little for sacrifices and all they implied, I found myself wanting to travel back with them by way of the texts.

All this does not mean that they went into the pages as one. In fact, they often argued about exactly where that text could take them. And that made it harder for me to tag along. It happened that night.

The text described a man who was about to eat a minimal quantity of his sacrifice, as mandated by the law. He took a mouthful from the lamb and an equal amount from the breads, both of which constituted his sacrifice. But what if one part of this sacrifice is ritually spoiled? It depends on when he eats it, the teacher explained.

Reb Eliahu, however, had found an alternative reading of the text. In his, this would be the case only under specific circumstances.

"If you want to say it that way you may; but I read it this way," Reb Yechiel Michl remarked, ratifying the Rav's interpretation of how things were done.

The Rav paused.

"Rashi," Yechiel Michl said finally, citing the authority of the great commentary on the page, "reads it as I do."

"But there's another version in the *Shita Mekubetses*," Eliahu argued.

"It can't be right!" Yechiel Michl cried, lifting the pen that he used as a pointer to keep his place. "It can't be right!"

"Look, why make it hard for yourself?" the Rav answered.

"With that version, the whole argument has to be changed; and then nothing will hold together."

"All the *g'dolim* [great scholars] see it Rashi's way," Yechiel Michl noted. He stood on the shoulders of scholar forebears— and with whom did Eliahu stand?

"Look, it's not too hard to see it my way too, and the majority isn't always right."

Eliahu was talking about the majority of great scholars, but he could just as easily have been talking about himself and us. There was no real distinction between the arguments on the page and those in the class. Then was now, and now then. The Talmud had always found ways of shredding and collapsing time. "There is no earlier or later in the Torah" was, after all, one of the primary organizing principles of exegesis. I had always assumed that that principle affected only the written page; but now, as it had in America, it began to dawn on me that the students of the text could become swept up in this same turbulence of time.

"And I say," Rav Moses announced, cutting short the controversy with a tone of judgment, "that you can read it this way and that."

The judgment, I thought, did not change anything at all. That was exactly where we had begun—with two versions of the line. But then there was a change; I could feel it in the room and around the circle. What had changed? Why were the men satisfied with a judgment that returned us to the status quo ante?

I had been using a little tape recorder in order to capture as much as possible in each class. From the start I had explained to the men with whom I *lernt* that for me each word they spoke was important, as this was what I hoped to study as well as the texts themselves. No one seemed to object to the little machine that lay on the table and swallowed up their speech. In fact, everyone seemed intent—at least, at first—on getting himself into the record. For Reb Zanvil this was something to be done furtively. And often I would see my partner on the left watch the little green light that flashed as the recorder took in various sounds to see if it would catch even his coughs and snorts.

That little machine allowed me to take a second look at the world I entered whenever the books were opened and the men gathered around them. Tonight it would help me discover what had been so momentous about Rav Moses' judgment.

When I returned home, I rewound the tape to find the moment when the little exchange took place. Carefully I wrote down all the words of the discussion and began to review them as carefully as my *chavruse* had themselves reviewed the sacred texts. And then I saw it. I listened again to the tape to be sure that what I saw in this transcript was what I could have heard in the class. I closed my eyes as I listened and tried to place myself back inside the room and at the L-shaped table.

Everything had been spoken in the present tense. What had perhaps for others been an archaic controversy between two alternative versions of an ancient text was for these men a fresh argument. They were not just citing divergent texts; they were almost composing them afresh. So finally, when the Rav arrived at the same judgment that the redactors of the text had reached generations earlier, it was not simply an echo of that decision out of the past. Instead, it had all the freshness and novelty of the original decision. The laughter I heard in reaction to his decision was the delight which these men felt in being able to work out their different opinions along the same pathways, the tried and true pathways of their antecedents. Even their controversies did not distance them from the world of the Talmud but rather kept them immersed in it. Only if I allowed myself to see the old as if it were fresh and new could I too share in the delight, could I come to care about sacrifices at the Temple.

The idea, to be sure, was not altogether new to me. Orthodox

Jews who try to live lives attached to the past yet embedded in the present often find themselves forced to overcome time in this way. For the most part, the effort is not made. Compartmentalization is rather the rule—where past is past and present present, and one simply learns to dim the lights in one room while passing into the other. Logic has nothing to do with it, and striving for consistency is avoided like sin.

But the Talmud class is something different. Here compartments collapse, and rooms open into one another. Anyone who does not accept this reality runs the risk of becoming overwhelmed either by the irrelevance of his texts—as I often had been in the past—or by the importance of the present. I returned to class the next night prepared to let myself into the past wholeheartedly.

I began to attend the classes at Shaarey Chesed every evening. After several weeks I was accepted as a regular in the circle, and when once or twice I did not attend, I was greeted with special warmth upon my return.

"We kept your seat for you," I was told.

In time, I too was handed a pinch of snuff at the beginning of the class; and when that happened, I had the feeling that I had penetrated the life of the circle. But while each week I felt a closer tie to the men with whom I shared this special hour every evening, I never quite got over a sense of distance from the text. There was little in the order of the sacrifices that could fire my imagination, and try as I might, I could not quite visualize the scene at the Temple in the same way that my *chavruse* did. Whenever I thought about the rituals and procedures, my mind instead pictured a slaughterhouse with the lowing of calves and the bleating of goats all being killed and seared and smeared. The holy priest with his smudge of blood on his thumb and toe, with his white garments or gold garments, could not inspire me with awe as he seemed to be able to inspire my partners around the table.

And then there was the Yiddish. While I was comfortable with literary or colloquial and conversational Yiddish, the particular syntax and grammar of Talmudic Yiddish often left me completely frustrated. My fellow students spoke telegraphically, like the text they were studying. They knew it so well, had reviewed its arguments and turns of logic so frequently, that they needed just a word or phrase to suggest an entire passage, while I was left behind in the wake of their review.

Occasionally I could follow the drift of an argument for a while, but then as the Talmud went onto one or another tangent or we reviewed a complex commentary of the Tosaphists, those great medieval exegetes, I would once again find myself behind.

But if I could not keep up, I could still stay in. Squeezed into my place on the bench, I settled for an experience that was different; I came for the music.

The men I studied with chanted the text. Theirs was not the sort of tune one could whistle or dance to; it was rather the rhythmic rise and fall of *gemore-nign*. This singsong had for generations been the voice of the Jewish people. So much had it infused their character that Yiddish, the *mama-loshn*, or mother tongue, of European Jewry, took on its cadences. In America, the Jews I knew had by and large rid themselves of these inflections. What was once the sound of a scholar had in America become the inflection of a greenhorn. But here, where the Talmudist was still king, these cadences were the sounds of royalty.

At home, sometimes even as I lay in bed, I would turn on my tape recorder and listen to the gently rising and falling tones of the *lernen* and imagine that I was a young boy sitting outside my grandfather's study listening to him review the holy books and feeling a sense of security in the knowledge that all was right with the world. It was, to be sure, an adopted fantasy, for I had never known my grandfathers, nor had I ever gone to sleep to the sounds of *gemore-nign*. But it sustained me through the cold Jerusalem winter and gave me a sense of belonging that I seemed to need.

Maybe it was my habit of listening to the tapes in bed or perhaps it was the opacity of the texts, but more and more I found myself dropping off like Zanvil during the class. What had so caught my fancy during those first days now became more and more routine, and I was losing my grasp on the proceedings. To be sure, I had been changed by the Shaarey Chesed experience. My prayers were now slower-paced, and I stopped to think about the meaning of all the words I used. No longer could I rush through the liturgy as I had done on that first night. I knew all the characters in the room, knew who would stand for whom and who was widely respected as well as those who ran after respect but never seemed to catch up with it. And I learned what it meant to be part of a *chavruse*.

But I learned about the limitations of my experience as well. As much as my partners were willing to accept me and as open as the congregation was, there were barriers of biography that simply precluded my staying within this world. As if by some sort of biological rejection process, the strangeness in me was forcing me out. More and more I found excuses for skipping evenings at Shaarey Chesed.

In time I returned to the circle there, and whenever I did I found my seat waiting for me. The men had missed me, but no one was ever certain how long I had been away. They, as I already knew, had a very different notion of time from mine. They dealt in eternities; I was stuck in the present. If I wanted to find a teacher and *chavruse* to fit my needs, I would have to search elsewhere.

TWO

A Torah Magician

SHAAREY Chesed had made an impression on me. It had per-
vaded me with the sense of well-being one can achieve
through a regular regimen of *lernen*. By my steady study of the
same texts that my forebears had reviewed for generations past,
I had entered the great chain of Jewish being begun in the
ancient academies of learning and had entered the flow of Jewish history. I did not want to give that up. The problem was how
to tap into that flow. Joining another *chavruse* at Shaarey
Chesed was not possible, for by doing so I would be publicly
rejecting those who had so warmly accepted me into their fellowship. Instead I began to search the little synagogues in the
nearby neighborhoods.

In place after place I found mere echoes of the circle I had
left. Nothing attracted me, and I was beginning to fear that I
would never be able to make my way into the Talmud. True,
not all of its pages were taken up with concerns over the sacrifices, but whatever else was there seemed always to be steeped in
darkness as far as I was concerned. Perhaps, I thought, I was
better off looking for a group that would lead me into Scripture,

whose stories and lessons still remained appealing and accessible to me.

But such a *chavruse* was hard to find. None of the synagogues I visited had one, and no one I asked could point me in the proper direction. No one, at least, except a grizzled old pensioner whom I had always seen sitting in one of the other rooms at Shaarey Chesed but with whom I had hardly ever spoken. Approaching him, almost out of desperation, I asked him if he knew of any place where I might study *Chumash*—the Five Books of Moses—in some intensive way.

Maybe I had never put the question precisely in that simple a way before. I'm not sure. Whatever the reason, I got an answer that day.

"You know you can't really *lern Chumash*," the man began, "without the *Torah sheh be-al peh*"—reminding me that the Oral Tradition embedded in the Talmud was indispensable even for what appeared to be a simple review of the Bible. He patted the pages of his open Talmud as he spoke. I looked down at it and away from his eyes. Then, almost as an afterthought, he added: "Maybe you could try Rav Krol."

"Who is he?"

"Oh, my friend, he is one of the last great *parshanim*. You will not find many teachers like him anymore. He is a *gaon*—a genius—who knows every commentary on the Bible by heart. Rashi, Maimonides, Nachmanides, Abravanel—all the greats. You will see: he is a Torah magician."

"A Torah magician?"

"You will see the way he calls the commentators from his memory and brings them to life—it is as if each of them were there in the room when he speaks. The voice is Rav Krol's, but the words are theirs. A real Torah magician."

"When does he speak?"

"Go to Ohel Avraham on Shabbos afternoon, after *mincha*."

Such a man must surely have a circle with whom he studied. I would go to hear him on Sabbath afternoon in his little synagogue.

The synagogue, a single chamber nestled among a small row of apartments, stood in the shadow of a far larger and more imposing congregation half a block away. Unlike the other, in which several hundred men and women could easily fit, Ohel Avraham—the tent of Abraham—as this place was called, could at best seat about a hundred and fifty men and perhaps half as many women in an upstairs balcony. Its size, however, was not what made the place unique. At Ohel Avraham it was Rav Krol above all else that distinguished the place.

He was not at all imposing in appearance. His beard, a salt-and-pepper mass of curls, was neither wild enough to fire one's imagination nor sufficiently groomed to catch one's eye. A small man, he was neither especially rotund, so as to look like some friendly Jewish cherub, nor emaciated enough to fit the image of an ascetic scholar. He wore a black frock coat and black wide-brimmed hat, but that was pretty much the standard uniform among many Jersualem rabbis. He did have a pronounced limp, which I later learned had resulted from a dramatic jump off a Nazi train that had been taking him to a concentration camp. But while the limp and the story of its origin might add something to his charisma, it was his teaching and not his biography that attracted his followers and disciples.

The sages had imposed upon the Jewish people a strict regimen when it came to the matter of reviewing Scripture. "Do not sit down to eat on the Sabbath until you have completed reviewing the weekly portion," they had demanded. And one review along with the reader during the morning services was not sufficient. As the Talmud in its opening volume explained, each Jew was expected to review the portion "*shnyim mikra ve-echad targum*"—twice in its original text and once more with translation and commentary. For many, only the help of a teacher would allow them to completely fulfill this felt obligation. Rav Krol was such a teacher.

I looked around. At the right side of the sanctuary, in an alcove that served at once as a library and as the *bes medresh*, was a table covered with food and drink. About it sat approximately thirty men. Along one side and behind the bench filled with people was a wall of books. Opposite was the rest of the *shul*, with its rows of pews. But the pews were far from empty. Instead, the section closer to the table was filled with more people, a kind of second echelon of participants who did not share in the food but who could share in the words that Rav Krol, at the head of the table, would soon offer.

The eating was the briefest part of the proceedings. A small roll, a piece of herring or *gefilte* fish and a drink of seltzer or whiskey made up the meal. It took just a few minutes to get past the food. As soon as they had done so after their few bites, most of the men around the table started talking or singing. Soon the singing overwhelmed the talk and the men began to sway to the rhythms of their song. A few clapped their hands or banged the table as they sang. Others, resting their chins on one hand, toyed with the empty toothpicks which in place of fish balls and herring now littered the table. Some slid their fingers or plastic forks along the tablecloth and made little piles of the crumbs which were all that remained of the rolls. Others drummed their fingers in time to the songs.

Those in the pews, set back from the action of the table, whispered to one another. A few leaned over open books as they did so. They were near the table but for now still separate from what went on there.

At the front Rav Krol, his head tilted slightly upward, had taken off his hat. His big black *yarmulke* was not velvet, like those Hasidim often wore; his was a dull silk one that looked as if it were filled with air. Every so often it seemed to slide back on his head, so that he would have to lift his hand and push it back into place, appearing to try to screw it on tighter. Above him, on the wall and near the ceiling, an electric fan spun quietly and oscillated from side to side, rustling the loose hairs of his beard and perhaps accounting for his slippery skullcap.

The rabbi was not singing. Neither was he lost in reverie or caught up in conversation. He sat instead with an inscrutable half-smile on his face. To some his expression may have signified his pleasure at being surrounded by men who, at least during these few moments, acted like his disciples. Others might explain his look as a reflection of the joy of learning which inevitably emerged from the constant dialogue of scholars that went on inside his head. No one had ever asked him to account for it. It was almost as if he sat there in a sort of suspended animation, waiting for his cue, after which he would spring to life and alter the nature of the occasion.

As I watched and listened, increasing numbers of men glided into the room. Some stood in the little foyer near the door. Others moved toward the center and the *bimah*, or altar, on which the Torah scrolls were normally placed during reading. A few stood or sat outside on the stoop.

As I looked at them, it seemed to me that during these moments before Rav Krol spoke, each man in the room would frequently and sometimes surreptitiously turn toward the Rav or seem to cock an ear at the slightest movement or sound which indicated that the talk was about to begin. Surely nothing else could explain the perfect silence and rapt attention that greeted even the first syllables the rabbi spoke. But then he too, as I discovered, was—however abstracted he might appear—keenly aware of the cues emanating from his congregation.

Two men, arm in arm, slowly marched in perfect step up the center aisle of the synagogue. One man whispered directly into the ear of the other; then the other whispered back. And only when both had taken their turns in the dialogue did they look each other in the face. Then they nodded knowingly and broke into laughter. There seemed an easy intimacy about the two that for a time made them apparently oblivious of their surroundings. The aisle was not especially long, and so their march cannot have taken very long, and yet the entrance of these two stands out in my memory, as if it had been carried out in dramatic slow motion.

The taller of the two—a man in his fifties and of stocky build—wore a big black hat, but this was not a Hasid's or even a rabbi's headdress. It was, rather, a stylish fedora with sharp edges and bent brim, worn at a rakish slant. To match his hat he had on a dark suit and tie, which distinguished him from the others in the room.

His partner, all in white, wore no hat but instead had on a very large and rather bulky knitted blue *yarmulke*, and on it in big white crocheted letters was his Hebrew name. I could see the outlines of his *talis koton*. His more pious colleagues wore the edges of those ritual fringes in full public view so that they might, in line with the divine command, "look upon it and remember to do all My commandments," but this man had left them under his shirt. As they walked in, the two men headed for the *bimah*. When they reached their perch in the center of the room, the man in the suit nodded and waved to a few of the others, while his partner leaned down and exchanged some words with the men nearby.

Their arrival was apparently a cue for the class to begin, for suddenly a subtle but unmistakable change came over the room. Rav Krol tilted his head forward, leaned toward the table and placed the fingertips of his right hand at its corner, seeming to pull himself closer to those in front. Then, with his other hand, he once again adjusted his *yarmulke*, sweeping it forward.

Without pausing, he let that hand slip gently and ever so slowly down over his forehead, eyelids, nose, mouth and beard. It was as if he were wiping his previous expression away and preparing to put on a new face for what would follow. By the time his left hand reached the tip of his beard, everyone seemed ready to hear him speak.

In a wave, a sea of faces turned toward the teacher. Those who had been out on the stoop and become aware of the sudden silence quickly and quietly slipped in through the door and now stood at the back, facing the table from which, seated, Rav Krol began to speak. At first his voice was hardly audible, and so a few men who had lingered on the left side of the *shul* moved across the aisle and slid in next to the last man in the pews at the right. The men at the tables all put away their toothpicks and forks.

"*Ve dibarto bom be shivtecha be veysecha,*" he began by quoting from the morning's Torah reading. Today the verse came from among the most famous words in Scripture, the first paragraph of the *Kriyat Shma*, the Jewish declaration of faith. "And you shall speak of them [the commandments] when you are sitting at home and when you go on a journey, when you lie down and when you rise up. You shall bind them for a sign on your hand, and they shall be for phylacteries between your eyes. You shall inscribe them on the doorposts of your house and on your gates."

As he quoted the verse, I could see many of the men around me whisper the words along with him. Mixed with their breath were these credal phrases which all of us in the room knew by heart. Softly, we recited again the faith of our fathers and demands of our God. We became echoes of our predecessors, the children of Israel.

Rav Krol paused for a moment. Again he rubbed his hand over his eyes. "Beloved are Israel," he began quoting the Talmud, "for the Holy One, blessed be He, has surrounded them with precepts."

And now his voice changed, as if someone else were speaking. "Rabbi Eliezer ben Yaakov said, 'Whosoever has phylacteries on his head, phylacteries on his arm, fringes on his garment and a *mezuza* on his doorpost is certain not to sin.'"

Easily, our teacher moved from the written to the oral tradition, from Scripture to rabbinic gloss. Rav Krol began to quote from dozens of commentaries on the verse. First came a complex exposition of the laws pertaining to these ritual articles. As the train of his thought rushed ahead, one rail of reasoning merged quickly with another and led to a third, a fourth, a fifth—until I was lost. Then he moved into legend and narrative. He spoke in Yiddish, his phrases strung together as if in a single unpunctuated sentence. I struggled to keep up. But I could hold on to little more than the stories.

"'Affixing a *mezuza* is a commandment which comes to us from this verse. And inside it on parchment are the words of this passage. But the essence of the commandment is to ensure that each person will keep in his memory a faith in God whenever he leaves or enters his home.'"

I got lost in the flow of his speech and then once again tapped into it. He had led us a long way from his initial verse. But in the end he would bring us back so that his closing line was identical with his opening one.

Now he was into the book of Ruth, great-grandmother of that most famous and revered of Israelite kings, David, forebear of the Messiah.

"And Naomi said [to her Moabite daughters-in-law], 'Return, my daughters. . . .' And Ruth replied, 'Do not force me to leave you and go back.'"

There was a soft pleading in his voice when he spoke the dialogue and then a harder inflection when he added the commentary. This, it seemed to me, was what was truly meant by the Jewish Oral Tradition. I kept up as best I could while Rav Krol continued:

"The Igeret Shmuel tells us that Ruth added: 'It is my intention to convert, and better that it be by your hand than by another.' When Naomi heard this, she began to review with Ruth the Jewish law. She said to her: 'My daughter, it is not the practice for Israelite women to go to the Gentile's theaters and circuses.' So Ruth answered her: 'Whither thou goest, I shall go.'

"Then Naomi said to her: 'It is not customary for Israelite women to live in a house which has no *mezuza*.' And so Ruth answered her: 'Whither thou lodgest, I shall lodge, thy people shall be my people and thy God shall be my God.' "

It was a simple tale with a transparent message; but spoken in the gentle voice of this old rabbi it struck me as strangely moving. I knew the story, but hearing it this way and in this place made it seem fresh and new. I was not really sure why.

From the story of Ruth he moved on to other tales and commentaries which touched upon the importance of the *mezuza* or phylacteries or fringes. These were the Scriptural themes of his narrative. But as with a complex variation on even a simple melodic line, only those with the keenest ear and clearest reasoning could follow every twist and turn in his talk.

"And I also see something else in the Yerushalmi," he added, quoting this time from the Palestinian rather than the Babylonian version of the Talmud. The glazed look that now passed over his eyes suggested that Rav Krol did indeed now "see" what he was about to recount. The pages on which was written the narrative he cited appeared clear to his inner eye, and I got the feeling that although there was no book in front of him, he was nonetheless not missing a single syllable of the sacred text.

"Artavan, a Parthian king and student of the great Jewish

scholar Rav, once sent his teacher a precious pearl, bidding him send back something of equal value. And so the rabbi sent him a *mezuza*. The king sent word and said: 'I sent you something that is invaluable and you send me something worth only a coin?' So the rabbi answered him: 'You are correct. My possessions and yours are truly not of equal value. You have sent me something which I must guard day and night, while I have sent you something which even when you are asleep will guard you, as it is written in Scripture: 'When thou goest, it shall lead thee; when thou sleepest it shall keep thee. . . .' '"

His voice was soft, and he spoke as if he were addressing only one other person, the listener. At first, each one of us seemed to lose his awareness of the others around him and felt alone with the teacher. Then slowly, as Rav Krol spun the increasingly intricate web of his narrative and commentary (which, now alone, I can no longer reconstruct), we got caught up in it together and one by one seemed to wake up once again to the fact that we were not alone. Then each man might turn to another in the room and share his enthusiasm or wonder at what he had heard.

"Moyredik"—formidable—I heard one man remark in Yiddish.

"Zayr shayn"—very beautiful—his neighbor in the pew replied.

And then the two leaned back and seemed to tune out, apparently satiated with what they had assimilated. Their faces appeared changed, reflecting the same abstracted expression that had earlier graced Rav Krol's.

Some men simply shook their heads in dramatic displays of disbelief, marveling over the teacher's capacity to remember the nuances of one or another commentary or the precise wording of a particular legend. And later, as I walked home after *ma'ariv*, I passed a small group of men walking slowly, immersed in a review of the complex line of the afternoon's teaching.

Now, again, I could no longer keep up. I had struggled with the Yiddish in which Rav Krol spoke and with those texts which to me were unfamiliar. Finally, when for a moment I let myself be charmed by this last story, I found that when I tried to get back into the stream of his comments, the current was simply too swift for me.

And then it was over. The Rav completed his thought: "A person has three partners—his father, his mother and the Holy One, blessed be He. His body comes from his father and mother and his soul from the Holy One, blessed be He. Only the commandments which surround him bind this all together. And therefore 'You shall speak of them [the commandments] when you are sitting at home and when you go on a journey, when you lie down and when you rise up. You shall bind them for a sign on your hand, and they shall be for phylacteries between your eyes. You shall inscribe them on the doorposts of your house and on your gates.'"

The men around the table began to sing the grace after meals, and the others in the pews slipped out to the stoop, where they began the evening prayers to usher out the Sabbath. I left with them.

The experience at Rav Krol's class had been riveting. I had seen a Biblical text through a variety of perspectives. More than that, for a few brief moments I had been able to sense a mind steeped in Torah. It made me want more. If I had remained largely part of an audience rather than an active participant in the *lernen*, it was still exhilarating to be within its boundares, and I decided to return.

For several weeks I went to hear Rav Krol's Sabbath-afternoon talks. Little changed from week to week except the line of his reasoning. But there was something in his calm ease with the verses that made me increasingly certain that I wanted to go through the Bible with him each week until I had completed the cycle. But I needed to do more than watch and listen; I wanted to discover whether I could explore these texts myself. "Provide yourself with a rav," the sages had advised, "and you will acquire a companion." "Provide yourself with a teacher," the great Shammai had added, "and avoid all doubt." I decided to talk with Rav Krol a few minutes before the next week's class and ask if I might study with him more intensively.

The days passed slowly, and I thought about going to seek him out in Mea Shearim, the neighborhood where I believed he lived. But I had no idea where to find him. Besides, I had waited so long already, a few days more wouldn't matter very much.

On Sabbath afternoon as I walked the streets toward Ohel Avraham it seemed to me that I saw none of the people I was used to meeting on my way. But then I remembered that I was quite early this week. Maybe, I thought, I would be too early and Rav Krol wouldn't be there yet. But I reassured myself with the thought that I could then approach him as he entered. At worst, I could stay late and then speak to him. There was nothing to be anxious about. He seemed dedicated to the idea of Torah study. Surely he would help.

The street seemed strangely quiet. I approached the building and stopped dead at the steps. Before me on the wall was a poster, the likes of which I had learned to recognize. A black border framed an announcement. I read the big black letters on the white sheet slowly and unbelievingly.

"The crown of our heads has fallen. Our father and the head of our family, the *gaon*, Rabbi Abraham Krol of blessed memory, the son of the great Rabbi Mordecai Nissan, may his memory be blessed, the rav of Ohel Avraham is no more."

I sat down on the steps and stared at the poster until I had memorized it. I closed my eyes. A story I had once learned came to mind and I could think of nothing else.

A student used to come to his master in the evenings to talk and listen. One night it was very late before he had finished asking questions.

"Why don't you go to bed?" asked the master.

The student bowed, and lifted the screen to go out. "The hall is very dark," he said.

"Here, take this candle," the master said, lighting one for his student.

The student reached out his hand, and took the candle.

The master leaned forward, and blew it out.

Once again I was in the dark. I would have to find my teacher elsewhere. I would go to Mea Shearim. Perhaps another Rav Krol was there to be found.

THREE

I Feel So Good Here, Why Should I Go Elsewhere?

"MEA SHEARIM"—the name is packed with all sorts of associations. It fills the mind with images of black hats and black coats; men with faces rimmed by hair and women with heads covered by kerchiefs, little boys with long earlocks and little girls with long braided curls never touched by scissors. Children are everywhere; each porch seems to strain under their weight. From out of school windows in winter and summer, their voices can be heard often rhythmically repeating lines of Scripture or sounds of the Hebrew alphabet. A father walks from the market, holding groceries in one hand and in the other grasping the small palm of his son. Mothers or older sisters push carriages behind which trail a gaggle of children. Insulated from the world around it, this is the heartland of present-day Jewish zealotry and headquarters of the "pious community," who look upon themselves as "guardians of the city." On the streets, the Hebrew of modern Israel is replaced by the Yiddish of Eastern Europe, and the order of an eternal yesterday reigns over the exigencies of the endless tomorrows that seem to drive life on the outside. And here I supposed I might find yet another doorway into the precincts of tradition and the house of study.

I already knew that this dense maze of streets and alleys with its many Hasidic currents and courts was dotted with small synagogues, or *shtibblach*, and houses of study. But I, like so many others who passed along the fringes of the community and got no further than its tourist shops, had never really penetrated into the core places of worship and *lernen*. A generation of assimilation during which our family had abandoned its Hasidic loyalties, when my grandfather—a disciple of the Bobover Rebbe—had become simply a memory, made the thought of my entering into the life of Mea Shearim anxiety-provoking. Surely my clean-shaven face, my short hair, even my knitted *yarmulke* would make all hopes for entrée vain. And as if that were not enough, my university education and the so-called "enlight-ened" mind I had there cultivated stood as internal obstacles to my passage into a world where a different sort of logic ruled. But still I would try. Mea Shearim held a fascination for me. I wanted to grasp something of it, however little that might be.

As I walked along Mea Shearim Street, with its gift shops, bakeries and little groceries, I knew I would have to find a way to get behind this facade. At the open-air market, I turned right and into one of the several courtyards which mark the neigh-borhood. To the left were shoemakers and butchers, their wares hanging out on display; to the right were fruit-and-vegetable stands. Beyond them were bookstores, and behind them yet an-other courtyard—one that few outsiders ever entered, for here there were no shops or stands: only synagogues, study halls and a *mikveh*, or ritual bath.

One wall of this inner courtyard stood out from the others. Across it were painted English letters which announced: "Zion-ism and Judaism are diametrically opposed." It was a curious sight. But not because of its sentiments, for these were by and

large characteristic of the neighborhood. Mea Shearim is plas-
tered in posters, messages as diverse as an announcement of a
pilgrimage to the tomb of the medieval sage Rabbi Shimon Bar
Yochai and an excoriation of the archeologists digging at the
ruins of the ancient City of David, south of the Temple mount.
All these signs were in Yiddish or Hebrew. This message, however, was something different; the way it was painted—in large
black letters against the blond Jerusalem limestone—seemed
shrill and somehow more threatening than anything else I had
so far seen. It seemed to suggest that not only were ideologies in
collision, but so too were the persons whom they inhabited.
Zionists—more, perhaps: modern Israel and anyone who was a
part of it—could not, I was to believe, pass beyond this wall.
And yet everyone in black around me seemed to ignore the
message and drifted past it and around the corner into the inner
courtyard. I followed, leaving behind what I could and opening
myself to what lay beyond.

There was indeed another world here. No trinkets or produce
attracted people to this part of the neighborhood; only religion
did. In the middle of the square was a large *yeshiva*, from which
came the droning sounds of young voices reciting Talmud.
Above it was the "Great Synagogue," the largest single place of
worship in the yard. Across the alley was the *mikveh*, from
which men whose earlocks and beards still dripped would
emerge in great numbers each morning and especially on Friday
afternoons. Next door to the baths was a maze of little rooms,
the *shtibblach*, in which one or another *minyan*, or quorum
for prayer, was always in session or being formed. Here one
could come at almost any hour of day or night and find men at
prayer.

I walked up the worn stone steps that led to the Great Synagogue. Around it were twenty or more rooms filled with boys of
various ages reviewing holy books. In each stood or sat a

youngish-looking Hasid who acted as their *melamed*, or teacher.
To reach the synagogue, which also served as a *bes medresh*, or
house of study, for the laymen in the community, I had to pass
by several of the rooms. A few of the heads inside turned to
stare at me. It was as if my presence invaded their consciousness.
Slowly, with hesitation, I walked toward the synagogue.

The voices of young boys reviewing their lessons rang in my
ears, blocking out all other sounds. An older man's voice would
cue them every so often and then the chorus would begin again.
It was late morning, and services had long since ceased. Still,
when I entered through the heavy wooden doors I found the
large room by no means empty. Several men were seated at long
tables along the sides, poring over volumes of Talmud open before them. As I watched from what seemed to me to be my
invisibility, an old story I had learned as a boy jumped into my
head.

Reb Zusya of Hanipol, the great scholar, once began to
review a new tractate of the Talmud. A day later his followers found him sitting in the house of study still poring
over the first page of the volume. They assumed he must
have become tangled up in a particularly difficult passage
and was trying to find his way out of it. But after several
days when they found that he was still immersed in the first
page, they were astonished, but did not dare question their
master's Talmudic skill. Finally, one of them marshaled
sufficient courage and asked him why he did not proceed to
the next page. And Reb Zusya looked up from the large
volume and answered: "I feel so good here, why should I
go elsewhere?"

In front of my eyes I imagined I saw this scene. Here were
men who lingered over and inside the pages of one or another

volume of Talmud, who sometimes ran through the complex arguments and commentaries and at other times wandered slowly and almost as if dreaming through their holy books. To the outsider such men often appeared as religious *luftmenshen*: "men of air"—Jews with no visible means of support. If one asked what kept them, they would often shrug their shoulders. Others, a bit more philosophical perhaps, might point to their book and then toward heaven, as if to say that they were supported by their books and held up by God. One man once told me—I think only half in jest—that he was planning a revolution, one in which the powers of light would gain control from the powers of darkness, where the kingdom of Jacob would take power from the kingdom of Esau.

I had already learned that it was futile to try to find their worldly ties. What made these men, what gave them their character and reason for being was their books and their *bes medresh*. It was what they lived for rather than what they lived off that mattered, and if I was to understand them at all, I supposed, I would have to tarry awhile with them. In the course of my wanderings around the synagogues and study halls of the city, I had come across a number of places that seemed to me to be places of such lingering. Now I had found yet another.

I wandered over toward one of the tables, my heart pounding. Here, more than anywhere else I had gone, I feared rejection. I thought of the stones that these men or their kin threw at drivers who passed near their neighborhood on Sabbath. I remembered the spitting and the contempt that often marked encounters between moderns and the people of Mea Shearim. But it was the story of Reb Zusya, which like a melody kept running through my mind, and the quiet scene of men engaged in conversation over holy books that at the same time drew me toward the table and eased my anxieties.

At the corner nearest me, a short, round man turned around. He must have seen something in me that told him what I wanted, for without a word he moved over on the bench and beckoned to me to sit down beside him. As I did so, he moved his book so that it lay on the table between us and pointed to the place from which the man who sat across from us was reading aloud. I tried to tap into what was going on.

The recitation was in Hebrew, but its inflection was Yiddish. This was not the everyday speech I had grown accustomed to hearing on the streets of modern Jerusalem. It was instead *loshn koydesh*—holy tongue—the lingua franca of generations of European Torah scholars. Studded with Talmudic and Biblical idioms, it was about as close to modern Hebrew as a Hasid's earlocks are to an Israeli's sideburns.

There was a rhythm to the measured rise-fall cadences. The tones at the beginning of each sentence would go up, and then during the translation and commentary they would once again drop down. Listening to the give-and-take, I could at first not penetrate the substance of what I heard, but I was lulled by its sound. And whenever someone had a gloss to make, the tune would stop and the rhythm was broken. But these breaks passed quickly, and the gentle melody and rhythms of the *lernen* were soon picked up again.

I looked at the speaker's face and was at once drawn to the mouth I knew was there but could not see. In its place was a fluff of mustache and beard which wiggled each time he spoke. Occasionally the tip of his tongue appeared and seemed to lick the hairs so that what might have been a word became instead an indecipherable grunt. And when the tongue was withdrawn, the soft doors of his mouth opened and shut so quickly that it seemed as if the vibrations of his beard rather than some unseen vocal cords and lips were accountable for the sound.

My partner beside me held the place with one hand and with the other stroked his beard. He held it with his thumb and curled its tip with his forefinger. But for all his abstracted grooming, the ends remained wild-looking and scraggly. A few hairs fell on his black coat and stuck there, as if in defiance of his attentions. From where I sat I could see his wrist and the watch he wore. At first I was struck by its contrast to everything else about him; a modern quartz seemed strangely out of place on a man who was clearly at home in a realm of learning that defied time. But then, as I stared at the watch whenever my attention wavered from the text and discussion, I noticed something that put my picture of him back in order and realized that the watch only *appeared* to mark him as a modern obsessed with a need to be precise about his time. I saw it when I looked at the date display. There, as I would ever after always find it, was the wrong date. It was not today that mattered; it was the eternal yesterday.

As if to echo my secret discovery, the speaker announced that the question before us in the text was the precise onset of the new moon heralding the beginning of the Jewish month of Nissan, the first of spring. How would its onset affect the rest of the days, ones on which the Passover and its practices had to be scrupulously observed? It was eternal cyclical time that concerned the men around this table, not the linear sort that modern men seem ready to count.

For a while my attention wandered from the discussion, and I looked around at the walls. There were murals on them, faded but still clear enough to be made out. In keeping with custom, there were no human forms pictured. Instead there were scenes that depicted Rachel's Tomb on the nearby road to Bethlehem and the Kotel, the remaining Western Wall of the Holy Temple. Around the carved holy Ark there were pictures of Torah scrolls with mantles of purple and red. And on top of the Ark were two golden lions of Judah with eyes that seemed burned in by coals. I looked away.

The rest of that first encounter with these men has largely passed into my subconscious, for what I next remember is our closing the books. I glanced at my partner and nodded. He smiled, and as he shuffled back from the bookcase where he had returned his book, he beckoned to me to accompany him out the door.

"Where are you from?" he asked in Yiddish.

"I come from America, but for now I live in Jerusalem."

"You like to *lern?*" He looked directly at me now.

"I want to *lern,*" I answered, "but I am not yet ready to do it alone."

"I have been at it for over sixty years and I also am not ready to do it alone." He chuckled and began to cough. "Come with me," he whispered between coughs, and then added: "Have you *davened mincha* yet?"

We were crossing the courtyard and headed for the *shtib-blach.*

"Not yet."

"So come."

Before we reached the *shtibblach,* I could already hear the sounds of prayers. And above them I could hear the call *"Min-cha, mincha!"* with which a new *minyan* was being gathered. We walked down the three or four steps that led into the alley and were met there by a man who grabbed us with his eyes and repeated his call. Pointing us toward one of the rooms on the left, where I could already see a line of men entering, he moved on to call others for the quorum.

My companion walked and I followed him to the little sink that stood in the alley. We would wash our hands first. Like so many other ritual ablutions, this one was—as I had long ago learned—not meant to clean off dirt. These waters were to be

used to put something on; they symbolized a spiritual renewal.
It was as if by pouring water over my hands I were giving birth
to new ones, freshly preparing these to take up a holy task. I
was handed the cup with which to wash. The left, the right and
then the left again—my hands dripped with water. I rubbed
them together, as I saw others do, pulling my thumb with the
palm of the other hand.

How strange this transformation might seem to someone who
had been watching me move from one holy task to another.
Why should one who has spent time in the Talmud have to
purify himself again for prayer? Was it the act of my having
closed the holy books and moved away from them that now had
to be redeemed? Perhaps. But if washing did not seem to make
sense to me now, I was nevertheless ready to believe that the
tradition does not draw its power from its capacity to mold itself
to the vicissitudes of an individual life; it is rather the individual
who can gain strength only by allowing himself to be shaped by
the tradition. So I washed my hands and followed my leader
into *mincha*.

There seemed an anonymous quality to the prayers here, as if
each man came not so much to be in the company of others as
to keep a personal appointment with his God. In time, however,
I discovered that there were many here who might be directing
their devotions toward heaven but all the while remained very
much aware of who was there along with them on earth.

In the alley, besides those assembling for a quorum, there
were some men whose intentions planted them firmly on earth,
for whom prayer was at best secondary. With each new *minyan*
they would move into action, while between the services they sat
on chairs outside. Some spent the waiting time reciting psalms
from little psalters with pages grown yellow in the sun and
shredded from constant leafing. Others chatted among themselves. Some simply sat idly and stared vacantly off into space.

These were the *shnorrers*—mendicants—who, lichenlike, attached themselves to the place, the people and prayer. During the *davenen* they would wander in, palms up, and shake a few coins in their hands. Some also held bills in the folds of their fingers, to tell their would-be contributors that larger donations were also in order.

But they were not there just to collect money; they participated in the prayers as well. When the congregation bowed, they bowed too. Each time the cantor would get to some portion of his repetition that called for a public response, the *shnorrers* were quick to join it. It was as if they were telling us all that they had not become so wrapped up in their begging that they remained deaf to what was being recited around them. Besides, they seemed to say, we are Jews like you; only earthly fortunes separate us. And thus they repeated, dozens of times each day, the verses of the *kedusha*, the sanctification, and the *modim*, prayers of thanksgiving.

I had become used to these ubiquitous beggars whenever I entered the precincts of Mea Shearim. Sometimes, when my older sons came with me, I would stock their pockets with coins so that they might get into the habit of giving. Besides, I did not like the harangues I sometimes received from *shnorrers* who judged my donations too niggardly. But the young child who placed a coin in someone's hand never received anything but a blessing.

Once, when my oldest son—then eight—came with me to the *shtibblach*, he placed a coin in the hand of one of the most grizzled of the poor men. A touch that would have aroused unwanted anxieties in me generated nothing like that in him. Instead, he stretched his little arm out and calmly set the silver coin in the old man's palm. The man stopped and turned, watching as my son looked to me to see if he had acted properly. I smiled, and then the *shnorrer* took his hand and placed it on the boy's head. Stunned, my son stood still as the man whispered a chapter of Psalms and then a blessing. I was not sure, from then on, who needed whom more: the beggars us or we them.

We prayed *mincha* quickly. Each man found a corner or piece of wall to stand near, and before long our silent devotions and public repetitions were over. The room emptied and a new wave of worshipers entered. Again I could see the *shnorrers* going into action.

At the door, my companion met me again. He touched my elbow and steered me to the right.

"You know about the *mitzva* of *hachnoses kaleh?*" he asked.

I nodded. It did not take too much time in my search for a house of study to learn about this practice of collecting funds for a bride's dowry. When I had first been asked for such money, I had wondered whether this request was just a cover for yet another ordinary touch. In many cases it no doubt was. But there were also the common cases of arranged marriages which depended on such publicly collected dowries. And there were men who took upon themselves the religious duty of providing for the poor.

"So, come with me and I'll tell you something more."

We walked through to the end of the alley and found ourselves once again out in front of the tourist shops. The smell of baking bread filled my nostrils. On the corner was an open-hearth oven into which masses of dough were being thrown to make large flat Iraqi breads. I would have stopped to get one if I had been alone. But this was not the Mea Shearim to which my companion, who by now had introduced himself as Reb Yosef Moshe Reichler, was taking me. We crossed to the other side of the street and under a sign that said "*Lechem Larevim* [Food for the Hungry] Free Kitchen." Here was the entrance to the *batey Ungarin*—the so-called Hungarian houses, known to many as the most insular of quarters in the city. I was, it appeared, to be taken in.

Reb Yosef Moshe invited me to follow him up the stairs into his apartment. We crossed yet another courtyard, where some of the children playing stopped to stare at the stranger; my guide remained oblivious to it all. His slow gait gave me time to look around. We were completely surrounded by buildings. Built about a hundred years ago in the times when living outside the protection of the Old City walls required the construction of houses that resembled fortresses, the Hungarian houses and Mea Shearim were really a network of courtyards. What once had been used to keep out Arab marauders was now a barrier against modernity, a shield the locals used to protect their style of life. Only insiders knew their way into and out of the many hidden passages that linked one courtyard with another.

Between one building and another hung lines of clothes drying in the hot sun. They afforded glimpses into life here. Most of the socks, underwear and shirts were white—signs of an attachment to simplicity and an obsession with purity; there were none of the pastels and prints or T-shirts that I had seen on the other lines that fill the working-class neighborhoods of Jerusalem. Diapers hung everywhere. Then too there were the ritual *arba kanfos*—fringed garments—hung out to dry. Some were marked with black stripes, in mourning for the destroyed ancient Holy Temple. They were of all sizes, for little boys and their fathers shared in this religious obligation.

Reb Yosef Moshe led the way up the stone stairs. He lived on the second floor. A hanging fringe tickled my ear as I climbed up behind him. A reminder of the commandments to be followed, a magic touch? Reflexively I felt my shirt to check if my *arba kanfos* were on. I felt the hard knots of the fringe against my ribs.

The door was open and we walked in. A small woman, black

kerchief on her head, greeted us. She smiled, and as she noticed my hesitation added, "Come, sit." She seemed not at all surprised by her husband's having brought home a stranger.

"You would like a glass of tea?" she asked after learning where her husband had found me.

I nodded. "Thank you."

Reb Yosef Moshe was already sitting at the table; he had hung his black hat in the closet and was resting. The climb up the two flights had taken its toll, and he was breathing heavily. His wife brought him a rag, and he used it to wipe the back of his neck.

We were in a tiny two-room flat. The room we had entered was a combination living room, dining room, kitchen, library and foyer. But its high vaulted ceiling made the space feel larger than it was. A long wooden table stood against the two windows which opened up on the courtyard. But the view from here was largely obscured by the clothes that hung on the line. Occasionally the breeze would blow the clothes so that sunlight broke through and illuminated the back wall. The shadows and lights made a circle on the wall, as if the sun had perfectly projected itself inside.

There was a small toilet off the kitchen, one that I later discovered needed a little help with each flush. A bucket stood nearby so that when the need arose it could be filled from the sink and then emptied into the toilet bowl. The bathroom was a later addition, for in the beginning, as I was to learn, all the inhabitants of the neighborhood had shared toilets in the courtyard. For bathing, the *mikveh* had always sufficed. And yet, somehow the place felt clean. Perhaps it was the stone floors, which seemed to gleam, or the smell of bleach and detergent that permeated the air. Perhaps it was the fact that everything seemed so neatly in its place.

My hosts, I learned, had four sons. Mrs. Reichler took me

through the other room, a combination bedroom and study, to the porch, which opened up onto the main street. From there she could point out where two of her sons were and several of her twelve grandchildren. They returned her waves. To the puzzled look of one, she replied, "A guest from America."

Her sons, she told me, had made her proud, but one for a time had worried her. He was a Bratslaver Hasid, a member of the sect that some call the "dead Hasidim." The Bratslavers are mystics, but especially unusual because they—unlike any other group—have never accepted any heir to the leadership of their sect since their founder, Rabbi Nahman of Bratslav, died early in the nineteenth century.

"I worried about him because he delves too deeply into certain matters. And he is also missing a toe—not a good sign. But God has been good to us, and the *shadchan* found him a wife. He is an unusual man. You will see when you meet him."

We walked back to the table. Reb Yosef Moshe had caught his breath. He poured the tea from his glass into a saucer and sipped it slowly and loudly.

"I will tell you something," he began.

"Sit, sit," his wife broke in, motioning to me to sit, and brought a second glass of tea.

"It was the war and I was very much afraid, so I had to do something."

"Oh, yah, he was very afraid."

"Yah, so I started to recite *Tehilim*," he went on. His wife laughed, and I too could not help smiling. Here was the old joke—in the face of emergency, a Hasid calls out: "Jews, don't just stand there and depend on miracles. Do something! Recite Psalms."—come to life.

"But still, it doesn't help. I still hear the shooting. And then I fall asleep and in a dream I see my father-in-law of sainted memory."

"He was a great scholar," Mrs. Reichler broke in.

"A very great scholar and a man of great charity. And when I see him, he is not smiling. So in my dream I ask him, 'Reb Tuvia, what's wrong?' But he doesn't answer and still doesn't smile. He just turns around and walks away.

"So when I woke up I felt even worse than before, even though the guns are not so loud anymore—or maybe I am just getting used to them.

"Anyway, the next night I go to sleep and again I see Reb Tuvia. I run to greet him, but still he does not smile at me. He turns around and walks away.

"Now I know from this that I am doing something wrong. So the next day—the shooting was over already—I go down and I begin to collect money for poor people, and when I have enough I give it to the people I know need it. We all know who these people are. I find them easily.

"A week, maybe two, I am doing this and one night again in a dream my father-in-law appears to me. Still he is not smiling. Again he turns around, but this time I run after him and I grab his sleeve and tell him: 'Reb Tuvia, why are you angry? I have been following your example; I have begun to collect for the poor. No day passes without my collecting. I seek out every poor person I know and give away all I collect. Why are you angry?'

"He stops for a minute and looks straight at me. He seems about to speak, but instead he closes his eyes very slowly. Then he walks away.

"The next morning I wake up and I decide that I have been doing everything wrong.

"You know there are four levels of charity. The lowest is when the one who gives and the one who receives know each other. In this case, the rabbis tell us, the one feels superior to the other while his fellow feels beholden to him. The next level is when the giver knows the recipient but he does not know the giver. The third is where the one who gets the charity knows who gives it but he who gives does not know who receives. In both of these the ties between people are made unnatural and coarse. But the highest level of charity is when neither knows the other, for here they can continue to face each other as brothers and sisters.

"I had been giving the lowest kind of charity. I saw all the poor and they saw me. It was no good.

"So now, after the last dream, I collect the money and I give it to the Free Kitchen or to the fund for *ha-chnoses kaleh*. Now no one knows who gives and who receives.

"After that, I see Reb Tuvia in my sleep again. At last he is smiling!

"So now that's what I do. I *lern*; I *daven* and I collect for *tzedake* and *hachnoses kaleh*."

He looked at me and stroked his beard, pulling it to a point.

I began to reach for my wallet, but he touched my arm and said, "There is time for that. Finish your tea."

"You have children?" Mrs. Reichler asked me.

"Four sons."

"*Kayn yirbu*"—May they continue to grow in number—she answered.

"We have been looking for a candelabrum with space for six candles," I said, looking for some way to make small talk, "but it is very hard. I have been able to find one with room either for five or for seven candles, but nothing that perfectly matches the number of people in our family."

"For us it's even harder," she laughed. "We light not only for each child but for each grandchild as well."

"But that must be a lot of candles!" I looked around for what I expected to be an enormous candlestick.

"Eighteen," she answered, and continued. "You see this

tray?" She pointed to a plain gray tray with rounded edges. I looked at it, half-expecting to find "Pabst Blue Ribbon Beer" printed on the bottom; the last time I had seen one like it was at a bar. "We fill it with oil and throw in the proper number of wicks. It is the light we care about, not what holds it."

"You see," Reb Yosef Moshe began, "it's the same with a *sefer*. A holy book can be worn, its pages torn along the edges, the binding not so good. But the light inside it can still shine brightly if you know how to *lern* it out.

"And people too. You look outside on our streets. Everyone wears the same clothes. They are black-and-white—not gay and light like the ones downtown on Ben Yehuda Street. But from the people with the dark, neglected clothes can come the light of learning, and from the people whose clothes shine but who don't *lern* can come a great darkness which covers their soul."

He chuckled and stroked his beard again.

I finished my tea.

"And where could I find a place to get the books from which to study?" I asked.

"You want to *lern* or you want to buy?" he answered.

"What do you mean?"

"There are people who want to buy *seforim* to possess them. They fill their shelves with the greatest scholarship of our people. On those shelves scholars, rabbis are engaged in the greatest debates, exploring the deepest and most vexing questions. But they cannot be heard; the books remain closed on the shelves. The bindings remain smooth, the corners of each page are perfect. The owners do not ever discover the misprints, the pages that have become stuck together. But they possess the books.

"And then there are others who are possessed by their *seforim*, who *lern* from tattered copies in some *bes medresh* but who hear each debate, plumb each commentary and discover the errors as well as the wisdom."

I thought of Reb Zusya of Hanipol lingering in his Talmud.
"But you cannot mean that it is wrong to want to buy
books?" I protested.

"Heaven forbid. But you must buy not to possess but in order
to become possessed. You must buy those books which you wish
and are able to enter. So you buy one *sefer* at a time. You *lern*
with it. You come to know it like a *haver* [a companion]. And
then you buy another, and so on."

He stood up slowly, and walked toward his hat.

"Come"—he waved to me—"I take you to Mintzer. You will
find books. Rachel, I will be back soon."

I finished my tea and followed Reb Yosef Moshe down the
stairs. "You'll come back on a Shabbos?" his wife called to me.
I nodded. "I hope so. Thank you."

As we walked along the street, Reb Yosef Moshe stopped and
talked to a few people he knew. Some handed him money. Sometimes he marked something in a small orange notebook he carried around. Other times he simply put the money in his pocket.
Always he ended with the Yiddish "*Zayt gebensht*"—be blessed.
It took at least half an hour to cover the block. He seemed to
forget my presence as we made our way. Finally, we crossed
behind Mea Shearim Street, past all the bookshops there, places
that sold trinkets and gifts along with their holy books.

"Not here?" I asked as we passed a block with several of
these bookstores. It was my first comment since we had left the
house.

"You can buy possessions here, and *tchatchkes*," he said,
pointing at the trinkets and bric-a-brac that adorned the windows. "But Mintzer loves his books. You will see. Come, come."

We climbed some steps that cut into a back street and from
there to a small block of apartments. Reb Yosef Moshe shuffled
along and I continued to walk silently behind. I had already
learned that there was no easy way to make small talk with him.

Besides, from his heavy breathing as he walked, I guessed it would be hard for him to talk and walk in the same breath.

It occurred to me that perhaps we had made a wrong turn somewhere, because there were no stores anywhere to be seen. Maybe my guide had become lost in thought and now we had wandered into some wrong alley. I was about to ask where the store was, in the hope of thereby reminding him where we were going, in case he had forgotten, when we suddenly turned in at a small building on the corner.

"The store is here?" I asked.

"No store. I told you Mintzer loves his books; he keeps them at home."

The hallway was dark, the name on each door barely legible because time had faded the ink on the little tag near each bell. They had, no doubt, been written in another era, when life here was new and visitors needed help in finding their destination. But people had been living here a long time, and by now anyone who needed to visit them already knew where they were. We climbed to the second floor and knocked on the simple wooden door. Reb Yosef Moshe was puffing heavily. I stood behind him, where I could see a little river of sweat rolling down his neck. It turned along his collar.

The door opened. A woman who I guessed was in her sixties greeted us. On her head she wore a heavy kerchief, which she tugged at with one hand as she held open the door with the other.

"Reb Yosef Moshe," she said, "come in. I have not seen you in months."

I was startled by her strong voice and demeanor. This was not one of the quiet, self-effacing women I had become used to seeing on the street in Mea Shearim. What other local woman would have greeted a man by name, with such familiarity and assurance, as she had?

Reb Yosef Moshe nodded—he was still out of breath—and walked through the door and headed for the dining room, where he dropped his fat body into one of the chairs. I followed him. The table was strewn with books, and the walls were lined with them.

"He's looking for *seforim*," he explained. "From America," he added in his telegraphic style, and pointed at me.

"Something special?"

"Well, there are a number of books that I need." I walked over to the table to look at the books, hoping to distinguish myself with my choices, but I was not at all sure what would be the proper books to want.

"These are Mintzer's own," my guide explained as I picked up one from the table. I blushed.

"It's all right. Please, look if you like," Mrs. Mintzer said.

"Let him look in the storeroom," Reb Yosef Moshe broke in.

"Go, then; Mr. Mintzer is down there. He will help, if you need it."

She directed me out the door and into the basement. Like all other residents, the Mintzers had their own *mahsan*, or storeroom. But while others filled theirs with old baby carriages, folding chairs and such, they had stocked theirs with books. Along with a study upstairs which was crammed with even more books, this served as their "bookshop."

When I walked into the basement, a darkness even greater than that in the hall hit me like a wall. In the corner one small door stood open, and I could see light coming out from inside. I bent my head slightly and walked through the opening. By the light of the single small bulb in the ceiling, I could see that the hues in the little chamber were all dark browns, blacks and blues—with specks of gold everywhere. But these were not the colors of the wallpaper or paint; they were the bindings of books, which were everywhere in evidence. Piled in corners, lying on the little folding tables in the center, stacked on the shelves, the books appeared to me like stairs to be scaled. There was a cozy bookish feeling in the place, a kind of island of warmth in the cold depths of the cellar. I felt immediately at ease, as if I would have no trouble finding the books for which I had been searching.

By far the most imposing of all were the large volumes of Talmud. Taller and thicker than all the rest, these tomes were the most ubiquitous of all the books. But they were not the ones in which browsers seemed most interested. That should really have been no surprise; most of those souls who entered Mintzer's knew their way through the Talmud well. There were few surprises to be found by even a cursory scan of its pages. Here or there, someone might glance at the quality of the paper, the clarity of the print, the strength of a binding, but there was no need really to linger over its pages in the bookstore. That sort of reading was done at home or in the study circle where *lernen Gemara*, the review of the Talmud, was carried on in earnest.

Those books that did capture the browsers were the *pey-rushim*—the commentaries—each one of which provided its own line of insight into the world of Torah. Written by both the living and the dead, these volumes offered glosses on every conceivable area of Jewish tradition and Scripture. Some men read them with the hunger that others might have saved for reading a late-breaking story in the newspaper, hoping to discover as soon as possible which if any new doors they could open in the mind. As I had already learned from my bookstore experiences, these were the treasures that lured men to the back corners of the room. And Mintzer, like all good booksellers, knew exactly where to place his *peyrushim* in order to move his clientele into and around his wares. Even in the small space of the *mahsan* he had left nooks where men could lean against the wall or a shelf and "taste a *peyrush*," as he would later explain.

Mintzer circulated among the few people who stood in the cellar, commenting on one text or another, providing its pedigree if that was necessary or remarking upon its originality if that was in order. As I watched him, he reminded me of an art-gallery owner who, noticing a customer's interest in one or another work of art on his walls, would saunter over to proffer some additional information and commentary about the object. For him as for Mintzer, the tender of information was, it seemed, a way of establishing a tie not easily broken between the customer and what had caught his eye.

A gangly man, Mintzer was over six feet in height and dressed in a long black coat. Even indoors he wore a particularly broad-brimmed black hat. In his late sixties, from all appearances, he had his earlocks tightly wound around his ears and neatly tucked under the *yarmulke* that protruded beneath his hat. Perhaps it was from having bent over books throughout his life, maybe it was the low height of the cellar ceiling or possibly it was some attitude that sprang from deep inside his character, but Mintzer had a way of leaning over as if to reduce his stature. His fingers were slim and long, useful for keeping his place during the study of Talmud and colored with the unmistakable pallor of the *yeshiva*. In one hand he held a small notebook containing his receipts and a plastic refill which served as his pen.

"*Shalom aleichem,*" he greeted me.

"*Aleichem shalom,*" I replied.

"You are looking for something special?" he asked me.

The time had come to distinguish myself. "Well, I need a few things," I began, suddenly quite sure of what I ought to say. It was as if the place had summoned up the answer from inside me.

"For one, I would like a *Sefer ha-Chinuch*," I continued, asking for a copy of a medieval text enumerating and commenting upon the 613 commandments which emerge from Scripture. It was a standard volume in any Judaica library, but I did not own it. With it I would be able to review the weekly Torah reading and discover its connection with the basics of Jewish law. It seemed a natural starting point for my purchases, and I knew it was a volume that an *am ha-arets*, a boor, would never think of purchasing.

"And then I would like a copy of Bialik's *Sefer ha-Agada*," I added, asking for a contemporary compendium of tales and narratives from Talmudic sources, a book that would allow a simpleton like me to track down the stories that others could find in the normal stream of their study. And then, with what I suppose must have been a subconscious flourish, I concluded:

"I would also like the Hofetz Hayim on *lashon hara*." Citing this famous treatise on the Jewish attitude toward gossip, I felt at last that I had marked myself as someone who knew how to appreciate a good *peyrush* and that I belonged in this place.

"Where are you studying?" Mintzer asked as he led me toward the books I requested. His pointed use of the word "studying" rather than *lernen* struck me; clearly he had already reasoned that I was not from the world of the *yeshiva* or *bes medresh*. My selections were simply too eclectic.

"I am here on my own, but I am visiting at the Hebrew University."

"Uh-huh," he answered, as if there were no real need for the details.

"The Hofetz Hayim and the *Sefer ha-Chinuch* I have here, but the *Sefer ha-Agada* you will have to get from Mrs. Mintzer upstairs."

"May I look around first?"

"Of course. If you are interested in *midrash*," he added, noting my desire to buy the Bialik, "I have a new collection of materials from the Geniza over here." He pointed me toward two orange-colored books.

Subtitled "Twenty-one Legends from the Rabbis According to Manuscripts from the Genizas of Jerusalem and Egypt," they contained legends and tales published from the find in the Cairo Geniza, the trove of manuscripts and old books that had been discovered during the eighteenth century in the loft of an old Egyptian synagogue but which still today was being plumbed for new information. I picked one up and opened it at random. My eyes fell on a fragment of a commentary on verse 26 of the 25th chapter of Genesis.

"And after that his brother emerged, and his hand was grasping the heel of Jacob. Why was he grasping? This comes to teach us that the kingdom of Jacob does not begin until the rule of the kingdom of Esau comes to an end."

I looked around me in this little cellar room, surrounded by the wisdom of generations of believing Jews. These books must surely now constitute the kingdom of Jacob. As I stood in Mintzer's cellar, it struck me that until now I had spent most of my life within the domains of Esau's kingdom and the only way that I could ever allow the kingdom of Jacob to begin was to free myself from the domination of Western and Christian ideas. They, perhaps more than anything else, kept me from becoming caught up in the way of the Talmud and in the traditions of my people. I would have to plunge into the world that until now I had only been visiting.

"I would like to take this too," I said, holding up the orange books.

I took my little collection upstairs and showed Reb Yosef Moshe what I had selected.

"So now you will have to find yourself a teacher," he remarked.

"Where? Who?"

"Only you can tell that. But perhaps I can point you in the right way. It will have to be someone you understand and who can understand you—that much is certain. Go to my son the Bratslaver Hasid. He has a good eye for what people need. Perhaps he will tell you."

FOUR

Show Me Your Way

INDING Menachem Reichler was not very easy. Although his parents had sent me to an address in the Katamonim neighborhood of west Jerusalem, when I arrived there his wife told me that he had moved for a time to a room in the Jewish Quarter of the Old City. "*Hitnahlut,*" she explained sheepishly. He was establishing a Jewish presence, "settling the land," reclaiming his heritage. Her husband had found a place close to the Temple Mount and was establishing his Jewish presence there. There he studied and sometimes slept, returning rather irregularly to their apartment in Katamonim. If I wanted to find him, therefore, I must go to the Old City.

The directions young Mrs. Reichler had given me were less than precise. By the fourth "turn" I had become hopelessly lost in the alleys and small courtyards of the Quarter. No one I met seemed even to have heard of Menachem Reichler.

"If you get confused," the wife had concluded, "go down to the Kotel and look back and up. From there you will see a roof with large spotlights on it. My husband's room lies behind and below those lights. Find your way back to them and you will find him."

I walked to the Kotel. It was late afternoon, and the sun had begun to turn the two-thousand-year-old stones of this holy wall a golden color. Most of the tourists were gone, and only a few people remained at the Wall. In a corner stood a man who looked to be in his late forties, all in black. His hat was pushed back on his head so that in prayer he could touch his forehead easily to the wall; and his feet were set one in front of the other, as if he had somehow been caught in the midst of taking a step. Back and forth he swayed, sometimes folding the holy book from which he read against his chest as he touched the Wall with his forehead. I could make out the sound of his recitations as I moved closer. The words were familiar lines from the Psalms.

"Serve the Lord with gladness; come before His presence with singing. Know that the Lord He is God; it is He who has made us, and we belong to Him. We are His people, and the sheep of His pasture."

Not all the "sheep" in this pasture were wearing black coats and hats. Slightly to the right of the corner sat another man. He too held a psalter in his hand and read from it. But his prayers resonated none of the assurance that I had heard in the tones of the younger man. The words came slowly and with difficulty. He seemed not to know precisely how to intone them: whether to speak them in the cadences of modern Hebrew speech or in the rising and falling tones of ancient prayer. The Hebrew he spoke was that of an Israeli, lacking the Ashkenazic accents that echoed in the prayers of all the men in black. On his head he wore one of those khaki-colored cotton hats that are easily folded up and slipped into a pocket. This one had clearly been recently removed and placed on his head, where it seemed to rest precariously. From beneath it I could see his longish gray hair as it curled about his neck. His shirt, unbuttoned to his chest, was white-and-red plaid, his pants blue. In his hand, along with the psalter, he held a black mesh sack in which were some fruits, a paper bag and a small camera—artifacts of another world which he was not yet ready to let go. He appeared to me to be one of those Israelis of the founding generation, men who had grown up as Jews in the ghettos of Europe but who had abandoned that way of life in the quest for a new Jewish spiritual and national landscape. Now that landscape had fallen into the shadows, while their childhood Judaism began once again to glimmer faintly in the light of old age. A few came to the synagogues; almost all at one time or another made their pilgrimage to the Kotel.

Between these two I found my place, unable to leave without saying my own prayers, and walked slowly toward the Wall. As always, I began by kissing the stones. They were still warm from the sun. In seconds, however, they became moist from my breath. At times it seemed to me that in this way the stones softened themselves and allowed my prayers to penetrate. I turned to the psalm I had heard earlier and repeated its message now for myself: joy in the service of God and the wisdom to know who is Master.

I turned to another chapter. "O Lord, You have searched me, and known me. You know my sitting down and my rising up; You understand my thoughts from afar."

I had believed since childhood in the efficacy of the Psalms. My mother had recited them each night since her liberation from the concentration camps. Even in the black night of those years in the camps, she had recited those she knew from memory.

"That's what saved me," she had always explained.

As a child, I had believed her; as an adult, I knew that her cunning and will to live had played at least as important a role in her survival. But the intensity of her belief in the power of Psalms had had its effect on me.

"Whither shall I go from Your spirit and whither shall I flee from Your presence?" the psalmist asked. "Search me, O God, and know my heart; try me, and know my thoughts."

I turned away from the Wall. The sun had dropped below the level of the rounded roofs of the Jewish Quarter, and I could see the spotlights behind which Menachem Reichler was to be found. Soon it would be dark, and I would have an even harder time finding him. The plaza in front of the Wall was filling a bit more now with men who were coming for the evening prayers. The old Zionist had disappeared; the man in black stood swaying into the corner, his feet still one in front of the other.

I walked quickly; the light in the sky was nearly gone. A few windows were already lit as I wandered about into alley after alley. At last I happened into a small courtyard which seemed to be just behind the spotlights. On one side stood the remnants of an old stone wall with a single small window in it. The limestone bricks around it were roughly hewn and uneven. They abutted onto a new building with smooth stones and a large arched glass window which opened eastward in the direction of the Temple Mount and the gold-domed Mosque of the Rock. A little garden had been planted in the yard. In one doorway, wedged in among the bougainvillea, capers and jasmine, I noticed a large blue metal mailbox. Even from a distance I could make out the name which in big red letters had apparently been hand-painted on it: "Rabbi Nahman of Bratslav."

There was no door, only a doorway, and so I entered. From the doorway I entered a tiny hallway, at the end of which was a breach in the wall. A large stone had been placed here as a step which allowed one to enter through the hole into another room. Someone had put a large wooden *mezuza* on the side of the opening. I bent my way through.

The second room, a bit larger—about twelve feet square—but still hardly more than a cell, was sparsely furnished. In one corner stood an old refrigerator. On the opposite wall was a bed, and near it a small plastic-topped table on which stood a little Primus stove. On the bed lay a big black hat, the sort Hasidim wear. Nearby was a weathered-looking wooden chair, probably one of those that had been placed near the Kotel for worshipers too tired to stand. Someone had attached a little shelf to the wall and on it were several volumes of *Likutey Maharan*, the writings of Rabbi Nahman, along with a prayer book and a volume of the Talmud.

Opposite the hole was a real doorway which led out to what was either a veranda, a tiny courtyard or a room without a roof. The Jewish Quarter is filled with such spaces which open to the sky and allow for the building of *sukkos*, the little booths Jews construct and dwell in during the holy day of Sukkos each autumn. Leaning against one of the walls I could see the remnants of last year's palm fronds which had served as thatch for the roof.

An old metal staircase rose steeply from the center to the roof. Narrow and bent, it seemed hardly more than a ladder; but it was securely fastened, and so I decided to climb it. The steps were far apart, and as I climbed my knees sometimes pressed against my chest. And then suddenly I was on top of the roof standing behind the spotlights. The view was astonishing. Because Jerusalem is built on mountains, valleys and layers of rubble, what appears from one side to be only one or two stories high can turn out to overlook a chasm on the other. That was the case here.

Below and in front of me were the Kotel and its facing plaza. The lights had already been turned on, and their yellow and orange blended to create a kind of man-made sunshine. Night seemed never to come to the Wall. A few people were still walking to and from the holy places. The muezzin had begun the call for the evening prayers at the mosque, and a line of Moslems made their way past the army checkpost and up the hill onto the Temple Mount, where the golden dome and deep blue tiling towered imposingly over everything. A light breeze had begun to move the cypress trees atop the mountain.

I scanned toward the south and the excavations there. From the Temple steps to the remains of Crusader dwellings, the relics stood silent now in the wake of history. A few people were lining up at the traffic circle where bus number one, which winds its way around the Old City and into the New, stopped to pick up passengers headed home after their devotions. Beyond, in the valley of Ben Hinnom, the infamous Gehenna where centuries before Jews had sacrificed their children to the idol Moloch by throwing them down the ravine, the lights of the present-day Arab village of Silwan were beginning to come on. With a moonless, starry sky, it would be difficult in a short time to tell where heaven and earth met, for the lights of the village looked the same as the stars. And in the distance was the Mount of Olives with its Jewish cemetery, from which, according to tradition, the Messiah would make his way toward redemption, bringing with him the newly risen dead.

I turned left toward the north and the countless domes of the Moslem Quarter which dropped in gentle ripples down toward the valley of the Kotel. Behind me, in a small tin shack, stood a single soldier, his binoculars pointed toward the Kotel.

"*Shalom*. Good evening."

The soldier nodded and smiled.

"Does someone live here?" I asked.

"In a manner of speaking. He's a squatter. Been here about two months."

"Not Rabbi Nahman of Bratslav?"

The soldier laughed. He knew as I did that Rabbi Nahman

had died in the previous century somewhere inside Russia. Nahman, grandson of Israel ben Eliezer—the Baal Shem Tov, who was founder of Hasidism—had been a curious figure in his time. A mystical and in some ways obsessed man, he had lived a short thirty-seven years. But in that time he had managed to leave his imprint upon a devoted group of followers. And as generation after generation refused to take on another rebbe who would become their new leader, Nahman had grown in stature. Unlike living rebbes, who, like all human beings, necessarily arouse disappointments, this dead rebbe—who lived on through his writings, the words of his chroniclers and the hearts of his disciples—had become an indelible presence.

Nahman had lived almost all his life in Russia, but for much of it he had been driven to make a pilgrimage to the Holy Land of Israel, a trip he finally accomplished ten years before his death. The journey—as he and his followers understood— required him to be moved not only physically but spiritually as well. To carry out what was really a voyage of initiation, he would overcome a variety of obstacles and experience all sorts of risks: a perilous sea voyage, bodily and spiritual degradations, insecurities and anxieties. Although at last he felt impelled to leave the Holy Land and make his way back to the diaspora, he believed the trip to have transformed him, cleared him of confusing thoughts, reoriented all his movements. And when at last he passed away, his followers—so the story goes—resolved to retrace his steps to Jerusalem. They broke the Rebbe's chair into a hundred pieces. Each man took one, and when at last they met again inside the Holy City, they reconstructed that great throne and placed it in the house of study where they reviewed the notes the Rebbe had left, the letters, messages and tales.

"No, it's not Rabbi Nahman, but it's one of his Hasidim," the soldier answered.

"Where is he now?" I asked.

"I don't know. He usually comes back after nightfall."

"Do you know his name?"

"No."

"Can I wait for him here?"

"Sure. There's a chair here if you want it." He pointed to a stool on a nearby roof.

"I think I'll just sit on the stones."

The soldier picked up his field glasses and continued his watch, and I settled down on the rounded roof behind me. Soon I tired of sitting and lay back watching the stars come out. In the distance the murmur of people praying was faintly audible. Time seemed to slow down, until suddenly I was startled by the soldier's voice.

"Seems to me your Hasid is coming."

I sat up and listened. At the bottom of the stairs I could hear the shuffling of feet. Sliding off my perch, I jumped down to the next roof and backed down the staircase. At the bottom, I found myself looking into the room through the opening. The Primus was burning, and a man in a black coat stood in front of it with his back to me. On his head was a heavy knitted white skullcap, the sort Hasidim wear underneath their hats. On the bed there were now two black hats, one slightly smaller than the other.

If there had been a door, I'd have knocked on it.

"Menachem Reichler?" I asked.

He turned toward me slowly, holding in his hand a small pot in which he was brewing some Turkish coffee:

"'Wait on the Lord; be of good courage, and He shall strengthen your heart; wait, I say, on the Lord.' Who wants him?"

It was a strange reply, and it stunned me. He had begun by quoting the closing verse of the psalm recited during the days of awe—a reminder that Yom Kippur, the day of judgment, had recently been celebrated. But he had ended with the common Hebrew response to an inquiry from a stranger. The result was unnerving. Did he mean who wants the Lord or did he mean who wants Reichler? And my answer, which was meant to be straightforward, became equally ambiguous.

"*S'licha?*" (Forgive me?), I said, meaning that I did not understand him.

" 'And the Lord said: I have forgiven as you have requested.' "

The quotation was from the Bible and the liturgy of Yom Kippur. He was sweeping me helplessly into his world of words with double meanings. I was at once frustrated and fascinated by this man who obviously shunned small talk and the simple amenities of conversation.

"I meant that I did not understand your answer," I tried to explain.

Again he played with my words. The word in Hebrew for "answer" is *tshuva*, but that is the same as the word for "repentance."

"My repentance is for the Holy One, blessed be He, to understand."

"I am looking for Menachem Reichler. His wife said I might find him here. I am a friend of his father's, and I am hoping for guidance in finding a *chavruse*."

"And who are you?"

"I am from America, but I have come to live here in Jerusalem so that I might find a way to study Torah," I answered. It was not the sort of reply I usually gave when people asked who I was, but for this occasion it seemed more appropriate than anything else I could think of at the moment. If his name and personal history were unimportant, then so it was, I supposed, with mine.

He turned toward the stove and shut off the flame. With only a small bulb remaining as light in the room, this made things darken perceptibly. Now he placed the pot in his hand on a little tile atop the table. Next he walked over to his bed and sat down on the edge of it. Unlike his father, he moved quickly and quietly; I could barely hear his black slippers touch the stone floor. As my eyes got used to the dimness of the room, it seemed to be that this man looked somehow familiar. At first I guessed that he simply looked like his father and the resemblance must be what had caught my eye. But as I walked closer to him, toward the chair which by his motions I understood he expected me to sit in, I realized that this was the man I had seen earlier standing at the wall and whom I had heard reciting psalms.

He was silent for a long time while he stroked his beard and stared at me and then, it seemed, through me. At first I had thought his beard was rather short, but now he pulled at it, and as he did so withdrew a knot from under his chin and untied it. Now I saw that the hairs reached far down his chest. He grabbed them and pulled tightly, twisting them with both hands, and with what was obviously a practiced manner tied them once again into a tight knot so that the beard once more appeared quite short. From his beard he moved his hand up to one earlock and loosened it. It too was far longer than it had at first appeared, reaching nearly to his shoulder. Now he rolled it up again tightly, tucking it up behind his ear and underneath his white skullcap.

"You know the psalms? 'Let me know Your ways, O Lord; teach me Your paths.' What does this mean?

"It means," he continued, without giving me a chance to answer, "that a man says since he is ready to bring his soul toward the Master of the Universe, he wishes to know God's ways and in this way he can continue to come closer. This is how Moses, our teacher, approached God when he asked Him:

'Now if I have found favor in Your eyes, show me now Your way so that I might know You.'

"But there are those who say that King David of blessed memory meant something more when he sang these words. He begged the Master of the Universe to allow His holy spirit to envelop him so that he might merit the capacity to comprehend the mysteries of the Torah, for only thereby can one come closer to God. The Torah is the way to reach the Master of the Universe.

"Have you gone to the university?"

"Yes."

"You did not learn enough there?"

"I learned a great deal, but not Torah."

"You acquired a great deal; you learned nothing. If you have come to acquire Torah as if it were one of the subjects you learned in the university, you will never learn it. The Torah is the way to reach the Master of the Universe. It is a pathway, not an acquisition. You will never finish it; you will never get a degree."

"I don't expect to."

"What *do* you expect?"

At a loss for words, I suddenly remembered a line from the psalms that I had recited earlier. "Search me, O God, and know my heart; try me, and know my thoughts."

He smiled and finished the verse from Psalm 139: "And see if there be anything grievous in my ways and lead me in the way everlasting."

He stood up and relit the Primus. "You know the meaning of this verse? It asks if there is anything in you that is willing to follow after *avoda zara*, service to strange masters—masters who would have you believe that the Torah is simply another possession, another 'experience' for you, a tourist site which you visit and then leave behind. And if such *avoda zara* is found it must be abandoned for the way everlasting, a way of Torah that goes only toward the Master of all creation, the King of Kings, the Holy One, blessed be He. You cannot leave this path once you have begun upon it."

"But surely the rabbis did not mean to place so many obstacles before one who would study Torah?"

"Are these obstacles? You have said yourself that you wish to be searched. You know that there are two ways of saying 'my heart': *'lebi'* and *'levavi.'* The first refers to the outer heart, the sort we show to one another, the one from which the love of one man for another can come. But *'levavi,'* the heart of which the psalmist writes, is the inner heart, the one into which the love of God may reach. That is what must be purified."

Like his father, Menachem Reichler was not one for small talk. We had plunged into matters of the spirit without any preliminaries. If I could not keep up with him now, there would be no reaching him later—or at least so it seemed to me then.

"Doesn't the verse say *'Ve-taher leebaynu leovdecha be-emes'* [Purify our (outer) hearts to serve You truly]?" I asked.

"Good, good. But that is because it is the outer heart that is filled with the lusts of human passions, feelings that get in the way of the love of the inner heart which the Master of the Universe demands from us: 'You shall love the Lord your God with your entire heart . . .' The outer heart is purified and only then can you love God completely. And how do you love Him?"

"You obey His commandments," I shot back almost reflexively.

"And the study of Torah is equal to all of these," he concluded.

While he spoke, he lifted the little coffeepot from the table and heated it over the fire. Now, as steam rose from the top, he removed it from the flame and once again placed it on the tile. Next he took two glasses down from the top of the refrigerator and filled them with the dark Turkish coffee.

"You speak of obstacles. What I have been telling you is to remove the obstacles that your life has already placed in your way. Everything else doesn't matter, for the Torah is 'your life and the length of your days.'"

I recognized the verse from the Bible.

My teacher, for that is what this stranger to me had become, continued without pausing as he took down a sugar bowl, poured a heaping teaspoon into each glass of coffee and began stirring them slowly.

"My rebbe, Reb Nahman—may the memory of this *tzaddik* be blessed—used to say that if a person cuts himself off from Torah, it is as though he were to cut himself off from life itself."

"But it is impossible to remain attached to the Torah day and night without interruption."

"Of course—the Rebbe realized this. That is our human frailty. We must eat, sleep, care for our bodily needs, carry on our business. But when we do those things we become grossly human. And it causes our inner heart to be in pain. So we fight this pain by blessing God for the food, the sleep, the bodily needs. We surround these gross acts with holiness to protect our inner hearts. Drink.

"Blessed art Thou O Lord our God, King of the Universe, by Whose word all things come into being."

He had recited his blessing over the coffee aloud so that I could answer "Amen." I whispered my own blessing.

The coffee was strong and sweet; its warmth took the chill off things.

"So where can I go to learn?" I asked, breaking the silence that had come with our drinking. "Your father said that you might direct me toward a teacher and a study circle."

Menachem didn't answer me for a long time. The silence made me feel uncomfortable, and so I made much of sipping my coffee, holding the little glass with two hands, turning it around and around and every few seconds raising it to my lips.

At last he spoke: "The Rebbe once explained that there is a difference between learning from a book and hearing the words of Torah from a teacher. The book contains words which are unattached to any human spirit; they are like notes of music silently written on a sheet of paper. Teachings from the mouth of the sage have a spirit and life, so that one who hears them feels immediately tied to the soul of the sage who speaks those words, just as an audience becomes attached to the one who sings the notes of music. That is why our sages of blessed memory instructed each Jew: 'Provide yourself with a teacher and get yourself a companion.' There is a difference between those interpretations of Torah a man comes to when he is alone and those which he uncovers in the presence of another.

"You are right: you must not *lern* Torah alone. The Rebbe also taught us that there is a soul in the world through which all interpretations of the Torah are revealed. That is the soul of the teacher. But to find a teacher whose soul can be attached to your own, you must find out first what is the character of your own soul—and that is not easy, because, as the Rebbe explained, anyone who wishes to understand the Torah must bring forth an interpretation from his own heart."

"And how is that done?" I asked.

"And how is that done?" he echoed. "The Rebbe explained that a person who wants to *lern* Torah has to begin by taking into himself words that are as hot as burning coals, words that are hard and fearsome to bear. These are not the words that come from the outer heart, the words of speech. These are the words of God—'God is the rock of my inner heart and the Lord is my portion forever.'"

I recognized the quotation as coming from somewhere in the Psalms.

Menachem continued: "But we forget God and abandon his Torah. 'Of the rock that begat you, you are unmindful . . .'"

"'And have forgotten God Who formed you,'" I finished the quotation, for I knew it. It came from the great song of Moses, his parting words to his people in the desert; and I knew it because I had often chanted that portion of the Torah in the synagogue.

"'And have forgotten God Who formed you,'" he repeated.

He stood up suddenly. "Tomorrow come again and I shall help you to find a way to bring in the words."

"Shall I come here, to this room?"

"No. Come to Katamonim, to the *bes medresh* there."

"When shall I come?"

"Come for *mincha*," he answered.

With that he turned to the bookshelf and took down a large book, opened it and began to murmur and sway back and forth. I set my glass on the table and left.

The next day I had no trouble finding the Bratslav *bes medresh* in Katamonim. Everyone seemed to know where it was, and I had to stop only two people for directions before I found myself standing in front of a large stone house whose engraved facade announced that this was the synagogue of the Bratslaver Hasidim. I walked into the large courtyard, in which a number of small children were playing, and up the few stone steps that led to a wide veranda which ran the length of the building. On Friday evenings, as I would later discover, this veranda became filled with the overflow of the congregation which squeezed into the place for the Sabbath evening prayers. Now it was empty. I had arrived early for *mincha*, and I found a few men sitting inside, leaning over *shtenders* reviewing large books which at first I took to be volumes of Talmud. One man sat slumped over, his face resting on his arms, which themselves rested across the open pages of the book. In a corner two young men sat, head to head, in front of their books, talking. One dug an imaginary ditch in the air with his thumb, while the other tugged on the hairs of his sparse beard. Opposite them, at the end of a long and beaten-looking old table, sat an older man, his eyes resting on the pages of a small volume of what I took to be the Psalms. His fingers played with the strands of his *tzitzis*—the ritual fringes.

As I stood there near the door of the room, a young boy of about ten ran up the steps, grabbed hold of the iron railing and stopped to stare at me. His earlocks, held tightly against his face by heavy-framed glasses, curled down from his crew-cut head to well below his shoulders, looking almost like pigtails. He wore a gaily colored plaid shirt, buttoned to the neck, which contrasted sharply with his dour expression and dull gray trousers. His long white *tzitzis* were held in place by his suspenders.

"What do you want?" he asked me in Hebrew.

"I'm looking for Menachem Reichler," I answered.

"Not here," the boy answered curtly in Yiddish.

"I see that."

"That's his son over there," he offered, and pointed to a little boy with red hair and glasses who like him had long curly earlocks.

Seeing his friend point at him, little Reichler ran over to us.

"He's looking for your father." The boys spoke to each other in Yiddish.

"He's by the Kotel," the son answered.

"I spoke to him yesterday and he told me he'd meet me here today, at *mincha* time."

"Maybe. But he doesn't usually come here until Shabbos,"

the son answered. It was a Thursday, and if the boy was right I
was a day early.

The boys ran off and resumed their play. I walked into the
building and over to the bookcase in the corner. It was filled
with volumes of the teachings of Rabbi Nahman. These books,
more than any of the others, looked worn and used. Some had
tape along the bindings where they had been reinforced. Others
seemed held together by just a few threads, while still others had
been rebound in plain red covers and were obviously living a
second or even subsequent life. As I stole a look around now, I
noticed that several of the books I had earlier taken to be volumes of Talmud were in fact volumes of Rabbi Nahman's
teaching.

I withdrew one from the shelf and found a spot at a nearby
table. I noticed now that a few of the men stopped to look at
me. Trying to look as if I belonged in the place, I plunged
myself into the pages. But try as I might, I could not decipher
anything beyond a word or two; the logic of the page evaded my
grasp, and I quickly found my mind wandering back to my
conversation of last evening. Hadn't Menachem Reichler told
me he would meet me here at *mincha* time? I tried to remember
precisely what he had said. I had asked him to help me find a
teacher and a study circle to join. In turn he had warned me
that this, while necessary, required me somehow to get in touch
with my inner heart, but that the only way to do this was to take
in words that were "as hot as burning coals." These would get
through to me and enable me to find the right teacher and
group. I asked how I could accomplish this, and—that was it:
he had told me that he would help me in the effort. The help was
to come here. But had he said he would be here?

I thought now about what his father had told me: Menachem
could point me to a teacher. Reb Yosef Moshe had never sug-

gested that his son would in fact become that teacher. Neither had the son suggested that he would be my teacher. Could it be that Menachem had sent me here to discover something on my own? If so, then he would not come here himself, and his son had been correct about his father's being at the Kotel.

I must have thought about these matters for quite a while, for when I looked up, the room was filled with people I had not seen when I entered. Almost all of them now held prayer books in their hands and stood facing the front of the room and the holy Ark there. At the left of the Ark was a window, and outside it were iron railings which at first I assumed to be the standard protection for ground-floor openings. But as I stared out the window, I noticed that the bar in the middle was smoothly cut, leaving a large gap right in the center. Turning toward the other windows in the room, I discovered that each of them had precisely the same break. I had heard many folktales about the "dead Hasidim," including ones that told of strange nighttime visits from Reb Nahman. Could these breaks in the railings be there to allow his spirit to enter even when the synagogue was locked at night?

Everywhere on the walls there were sayings from the writings of Rabbi Nahman: "There is really no such thing as despair"; "It is a great *mitzva* constantly to be joyful"; "Talking with God is the highest concept and greater than all else"; "Wherever I go, I am always on my way to the Land of Israel."

"Is it possible to pray to the Lord with words alone?" Reb Nahman had once asked. The Bratslaver Hasidim had answered his question by praying tonight swiftly and in an overwhelming silence. On Sabbaths, as I would later discover, they prayed long and loudly, with melody after melody. And there was dancing, too—but that would come later. Tonight, the men had entered so quietly that I had not noticed them. In similar fashion they had organized themselves for prayer. Now, silently, some men left the synagogue while others resumed their studying.

Menachem Reichler was nowhere to be found. What had he sent me here to see? I wondered. Would there be a *chavruse* that met between *mincha* and the evening prayers of *ma'ariv*? Was that what he had sent me here to join?

A few men settled around a table in the rear of the room. A circle was about to be formed. They were all Hasidim. Standing near the door, I wondered whether or not they would even acknowledge my presence with a glance. For some reason, I doubted they would. I was wrong.

One man tapped his hand on the bench twice and looked at me. It was a signal for me to be seated there. I came over and he moved slightly to let me sit near him. He handed me a book, a volume of Reb Nahman's stories. Even before this occasion, I had heard about these stories, some of which had been translated by Martin Buber, that great Jewish mystic and scholar of the previous generation. Others had more recently been translated and edited for the English reader. More and more university scholars were analyzing them. Now, however, I would study them in their natural environment, a circle of Reb Nahman's Hasidim.

One man began to read the text aloud as the others followed along in their books. He was a large man with a salt-and-pepper beard. His eyes seemed to sparkle as he read from the book, and every so often he would stop and sigh with a kind of obvious display of pleasure, as if he were being refreshed by what he read. At first the form of our review of the text appeared to be the same as in countless other classes I had observed and in which I had participated over the years: one man read and explicated a text while others followed, cued and echoed him, occasionally asking questions or making comments about what was read. There were digressions, too, along one or another tangent. But as I listened and watched, I discovered that there was something different about this circle. It was hard to identify or isolate in specific actions or words, but I soon came to feel that the words I listened to were not being treated like a sacred text but rather were being read as if they were a letter from someone. Often the reader would preface his reading by saying in Yiddish, *"Der Rebbe zugt"*—the Rebbe says. And when he said this, he made it sound as if he had just heard the Rebbe say these words, as if the echo were still sounding in his ears and could resonate in ours.

The words seemed to flow past me, as they had before when I tried to look through a volume on my own. I could not imagine myself a Hasid of Reb Nahman, and besides, I also could not rid myself of the feeling of expectation, the assumption that something unusual was going to suddenly happen to me that would startle me and break through to me and make me come to some great realization of precisely what it was I should do next. All the miracle tales about Hasidim and the eeriness of my visit the night before had created a situation that hardly allowed me to make my way into what I was hearing.

"You are not letting the words into your inner heart," I imagined that Menachem would have explained had he been there and witnessed my anxiety. Was that, perhaps, the problem—my resistance? Perhaps Menachem had really sent me here to allow me to discover that I could not find my *chavruse* among the Bratslaver Hasidim. I was, after all, an outsider and knew that I had no intention of leaving behind my own world and taking up the customs and trappings of these people. It was one thing to have a spiritual conversation for an evening with a Hasid in a dark room overlooking the Temple Mount; it was quite another to take up that sort of life. I wanted to be exposed to Jewish learning, to enter a circle of students, to find myself a teacher and gain companions, to understand and share in the world of Jewish learning. I didn't want to be a Bratslaver Hasid—or any kind of Hasid.

"If you believe yourself capable of destruction, then believe you are capable of repair." The line from the text startled me from my reverie. I thought I hadn't been listening or following, and suddenly here was something that had penetrated my consciousness.

I hadn't meant to do so, but almost instinctively I responded: "And how does one carry out the repair?"

Everyone turned to look at me. Perhaps they too hadn't expected me to speak. After all, strangers usually make their way into study circles gradually. Only after repeated visits, when people have had a chance to get acquainted away from the table of learning, do strangers commonly become insiders, able to participate fully in the life of the *chavruse*. I knew all that well enough from my experiences *lernen* elsewhere. Yet here I was, having breached the norm. My question was not to be ignored; in the world of the Hasidic mystic, extraordinary occurrences like the outburst of a stranger were not to be overlooked.

My ears burned, and I knew at once that I must have become red-faced. Inside, I trembled even more. How unlike myself I felt—I who was always self-confident, who lectured in front of strangers of all sorts all the time. Yet here in front of about ten totally unremarkable Hasidim, I felt anxious and unable to contain my anxieties. I looked to the windows for a moment and wished I could fly out through the break in the bars.

A song began to sing itself in my mind, and now I became conscious of it. As I thought about the words—roughly translated: "The entire world is but a narrow bridge, but what is essential is not to be afraid"—I realized that they themselves came from the letters of Rabbi Nahman to his disciples. Was this what had come in through the window?

All of this must have happened in a moment, for I cannot imagine that we sat very long in silence, my partners in the circle staring at me.

"It depends what it is that one needs to repair—himself or the world?" the man who had been leading the reading replied. "Repair, however, must always begin with the person himself, for only when we are all repaired and made whole can we hope to make over the world."

"And how is that to be done?" I whispered. I didn't want to ask any more, but I felt committed to my question; I had to see it through to its end.

"Sometimes it requires one to grow, and at other times a person must diminish himself. *Lemoshol*, for example," he went on, drawing a parable. "There were once two men—one very well educated, who had studied at many universities and written many books, and the other very simple, who could barely read the alphabet or the prayers. Both had come to a *zaddik* on the eve of Yom Kippur to ask how they could repent—that is, how they could repair themselves.

"When the educated man came, the *zaddik* was at his morning prayers, wearing his *talis* and *t'filin*. At first he paid little attention to his visitor but stayed wrapped up in his prayers. But when he had finished his meditations, he motioned to the man to approach. As he did so, the *zaddik* was just removing the *t'filin* from his head.

"'Do you see these *t'filin?*' he asked the educated man. 'They are perfectly shaped so that each corner is sharp, and inside, each of the four chambers is equally proportioned, holding the holy words of the Torah. The outside is perfectly black, as it should be, and the stems of the letter *shin* [the first letter of "Shadai," one of God's names] are etched beautifully on both sides. Whenever I look at these *t'filin*, I become inspired and stand in awe of the Creator Who has commanded me to place them as frontlets between my eyes.

" 'But do you know how these beautiful and inspiring *t'filin* began? Have you ever seen them being made? They begin as a single piece of fatty skin from a cow—white, soft, pale and terribly odorous. For a long time the skin is stretched over a cast of four forms. And when at last it is removed, there are four bulges in it and it looks even uglier than before. The odor is worse, for the skin is old and it has been stretched beyond recognition. Now it is ignored, placed off somewhere to the side. Thus left alone, it begins to shrivel up and draw together until at last the bulges are little more than nearly flat panels which harden into their shapes. Then three plates are placed between these panels to keep them from fusing together, while all the while the skin grows tighter and tighter. The large fatty skin with its bulges diminishes itself until it has become a small box, from which the plates are withdrawn with difficulty. At last the edges are pressed into a square shape, and the skin is made even smaller.

" 'Now comes someone who scrapes off a part of the exterior of the hardened shell. And as he does so, he carves the letter *shin*, the initial of God, upon it. And when it is thus prepared and shrunken from its former self, a scribe comes along and places inside it the holy words of Torah and paints it perfectly black and affixes the straps to it. And now it is no longer the skin of a cow or something that may be thrown off to a side or ignored. Rather it becomes something to be blessed, an instrument of devotion and prayer, sharing in the greatest of all holinesses.

" 'This all comes about because it has allowed itself to be shaped, stretched and then contracted. Then at last may the holy content be placed inside.

" 'So too must you allow yourself to be stretched, shaped and diminished. Then you will be able to have holy content placed inside you and the initial of God placed upon you.'

"Now, when the simple man came to the *zaddik* and asked him how to become repaired, the *zaddik* looked at him and said simply: 'Study at least one law from the Book of Codes each day.' In this way the man would become educated in the ways of his Creator.

"So you see, for some people repair requires them to shrink from what they have been before the holy spirit can enter them, while others must fill themselves up slowly and gradually from the fountain of Torah until they have grown sufficiently."

He closed his book, and with that so too did the others. Someone recited the *Kaddish*, the memorial prayer, as was customary when ten or more men ended a study session. Then, after each man took his book to the shelf, he returned to the others, who formed a standing circle near the table at which they had just studied. Slowly at first and then a bit faster they danced, singing softly: *"Ve-taher leebaynu leovdecha be-emes"* —Purify our hearts to serve You truly.

I could not bring myself to join in the circle, until one man broke the chain and reached out to me. Then I too joined this strange shuffling dance.

I left feeling confused. Was this supposed to point the way for me? Was I the educated man who had to be diminished or the simple one who had to be pumped up with laws and commandments? As I walked through the streets of Jerusalem back to my apartment, my mind wandered back to my thoughts of earlier that evening, and I wondered again whether I was ready to become a Bratslaver Hasid.

As I left the *bes medresh*, one of the Hasidim had handed me a little sheet of paper. Now I stopped under a streetlamp and looked at it. On it was a drawing of a crown, the sort I had often seen on holy Arks or Torah-scroll mantles. Along what was supposed to be the headband were written in Hebrew the words "*keter Torah*"—the crown of Torah. As I looked at the picture I noticed suddenly that what looked like a simple crown, however, was really the Hebrew letters *bet, raysh, samech, lamed* and *bet,* which spelled out the name "Breslov"—the Hebrew pronunciation of Bratslav. Bratslav superseded, or at least was, the crown atop the *keter Torah.*

Under the crown was written the following: "It is a great remedy and a measure of repair recommended to us by the holy *zaddik,* Rabbi Nahman of Bratslav, may his merits protect us, to recite these ten chapters of Psalms." Underneath, someone had written in: "This is a wonderful remedy for every sort of problem."

I needed another visit with Menachem. I would go again the next night—Sabbath evening—to Bratslav.

FIVE

Sabbath

LATE Friday afternoon. The siren announcing the last minute before the onset of Sabbath into this holiest of Jewish cities had just blown, and I was on my way to the synagogue of the Bratslaver Hasidim in Katamonim. Like many of the Jews I passed on the street, I wore a long-sleeved white shirt with sleeves rolled up to the elbow. My regular blue knitted *kippah* had been replaced by a pure white knitted one in honor of the Sabbath, my blue jeans by blue double-knits, my weekday sandals by shoes and socks. I had chosen to leave my prayer book at home, because it didn't contain all the special prayers that I supposed would be recited in the Hasidic service; I would have to use one of those on the shelf there in the *shul*.

The walk from my apartment to my destination in Katamonim was, in Jerusalem terms, a long one. Most people find a place to pray no more than five or at most ten minutes from where they live; to reach Bratslav would take me closer to twenty or twenty-five. It would be too far for my children to go, I thought, so I went alone. As I walked, I passed into and out of the orbits of several synagogues. Crossing one street or another,

I would find that while a moment before everyone had been coming toward me, now everyone appeared suddenly to be walking
in the same direction as I, and I knew by this that I had tra-
versed yet another orbit. Then, as I followed, those in front
turned off at one alley or another or into a doorway to their *shul*
while I continued on to mine.

That first Friday evening the trip seemed to stretch forever,
especially because as I walked I could already hear the sounds
of the afternoon prayers from the windows of the *shuls* I passed.
Afraid of missing the beginning of the Sabbath, I quickened my
pace, and little beads of sweat formed on my neck. When at last
I reached the outer fringes of Katamonim, the freshness of my
shower had given way to a clammy anxiety mixed in with a
sense of anticipation. I was going to confront Menachem again,
and that would not be easy.

Near me were some Hasidim obviously on their way to the
synagogue. I walked as fast as I could to catch up with them,
supposing they were part of the Bratslav congregation; but by
the time I reached them, they too were turning in somewhere
else. Either I was too early for the Bratslav crowd or else they
were coming from somewhere else.

Finally, I was there. A few people walked up the steps ahead
of me, but even from a distance I could see that the place was
already full. Yet what greeted my eyes was not at all what I had
expected. Had I witnessed Hasidim flying in the air, I think I'd
have been less surprised. After my encounter with Menachem
Reichler, to say nothing of my weekday visit here, I was expecting to experience something at the very least bordering on the
mystical. But nothing I had seen or learned about Bratslav
prepared me for what I saw. The room inside the building was
clogged, with some people already assembling on the veranda,
while the children chased one another all over the courtyard.
But the children were not Hasidim, and neither were the people

on the veranda or those inside. Everyone looked like me. Of course their faces were different, but their white shirts and knitted skullcaps, their clipped hair and naked faces marked them as the modern Jews they were.

For a moment I imagined I had made a mistake. Confused by all the turns and shaken up by my anxieties, I thought I must have walked into the wrong synagogue. But when I glanced up at the portico, the engraved lettering reassured me that there was no mistake: I was at the home of Bratslav in Katamonim. Where were the Bratslaver Hasidim? Squeezing through the crowd of people who stood near the door, I managed to find a little breathing room inside and a place to stand. Scanning the space, I saw a few Hasidim who stood out like penguins in the snow among the white shirts and knitted skullcaps. But these were not the men I had met the night before. These Hasidim were boys—perhaps the sons of those with whom I had *lernt* during the week, but without doubt not they. Of the hundred or more people packed into the small chamber, the Hasidim numbered at best little more than a bare *minyan*.

"Sam!"

At the sound of a familiar voice calling my name, I turned around.

"What are you doing here?"

It was a friend from the States.

I murmured something about wanting to pray with Hasidim.

"Well, you picked the right place," he replied. "This is the best show in town."

"What do you mean?" I asked, still confused by the sight of so many non-Hasidim in this place.

"The singing here is terrific. You'll see. It's real *lebedik*. Wait till you see this place come to life."

"But where are the Bratslaver Hasidim?" I asked.

"Oh, they're here. There're only about one or two families here. But they have gobs of kids, so it seems there are more than there really are."

"More? The place seems filled with everything *but* Hasidim; where are they now? These people all look like you and me—not Hasidim."

"That's not the half of it. Lots of the people you see here are nothing near Orthodox. Some know very little about *Yiddishkeit* but come for the high of a real Hasidic songfest."

I looked around while he talked and I could begin to make out these people in the crowd. To synagogue insiders like my friend and me, these outsiders—the newly or temporarily religious—stood out as clearly as did the few Hasidim in the room. Either they held new prayer books which they had obviously seldom cracked open—the pages were crisp and new, and only a few looked ruffled—or they wore their white shirts over a bare chest, without even a shadow of *tzitzis* underneath. They had on sneakers while everyone else wore shoes or sandals. They wore beards—which was fine—but coupled with long hair —which was not. And later, when the singing began, these people distinguished themselves by jumping around with displays of practiced ecstasy, often at the wrong places in the service or with just a little too much expression. They lacked that calm exterior, the matter-of-fact sort of devotion which the truly inspired seem able to project.

"But I've been here during the week and there were no outsiders. And the Hasidim I saw were different," I protested. "Besides, if this is going to be a Hasidic songfest, how can there be so few Hasidim?"

"I don't know what you saw during the week, because the show is only on Friday night. But I do know that a lot of the locals either go to the Kotel for Shabbos—they have their own *minyan* in the first alcove near the wall—or else they go to the big Bratslaver *yeshiva* in Mea Shearim.

"But don't worry, there'll be more Hasidim. They're just late because they usually rush to the *mikveh* in the last minute before Shabbos. They want to come in dripping with purity. You'll see them come in still rolling their *peyos*, trying to dry the hair and set the curls all at once. Too bad they haven't discovered curling irons.

"And don't be misled by your eyes. Not everyone here is an outsider to this scene. Inside some of these characters are Hasidim just waiting to come out. After all, that's why *we're* here—you and me. Right?"

As we spoke, a young Hasid pushed his way through the door and almost on cue began to roll the hair of his earlocks between two fingers, shaking the water out at the ends and twisting the hair so that it would dry in a curl. It was a curious movement, at once sensuous and mundane, practiced and matter-of-fact.

"Where will he sit?"

"Don't worry. First of all, even though we outnumber the Hasidim here, everybody understands that they're the hosts and we're just guests. Someone will make room on a bench if he wants to sit down. Probably, though, he'll go in the back room and wash his hands and then either stay there or else pull a chair from God knows where and find himself a corner that no one seems to have noticed."

Sure enough, the boy went to a small door near the front of the room, opened it and took out a chair, for which he found a small space near the wall.

My friend tapped my shoulder. "Here comes Nahman. If he *davens*, you'll be in for a real treat."

Nahman—a man in his fifties—was one of the few older Hasidim present tonight. He had on one of the golden coats that all married Bratslavers wore on the Sabbath. As he walked in, he carefully folded the right side over the left across his chest, and tightened the *gartel* around his waist. It was an ancient procedure by which Hasidim separate what they refer to as "the higher and lower regions" of the body—a separation spiritually required for those who would enter the sanctuary of prayer. Nahman's reddish hair was still a little wet, presumably from the *mikveh*, but his face had a kind of radiance which immediately and suddenly filled the room as he entered. A toothy smile sparkled from inside his curly red beard, on which little droplets of water still hung, while his ruddy cheeks shone. I couldn't figure out at that moment just what it was about him that so struck me. Maybe it was his black eyes, which seemed to meet everyone else's straight on, or the way he held his hands, as if they were taking in everything he saw. Whatever it was, it made his presence undeniable.

Even had my friend not pointed him out to me, I think I would have noticed him, for when he entered, a kind of electricity flowed through the room. People turned to look at him. Although, as I would later learn, Nahman almost always led the Friday-evening services, each week there would be a kind of quiet anxiety until he appeared, for fear that he might not come in time to lead and someone else would have to stand in— someone who lacked the magic he seemed to have.

For a time, during the winter rains, his father, who normally led the Bratslav *minyan* at the Kotel on Friday nights, would stay in Katamonim and take Nahman's place. Although he often sang the same tunes, there was something impalpably but un- mistakably missing when the old man took over. But when Nahman took off his *shtreimel*—the fur hat he wore—straight- ened his white woolly skullcap and donned a *talis*, the crowd seemed visibly to relax and ready themselves to greet the seren- ity and joy of Sabbath.

"Nahman": the name was, of course, the same as the

Rebbe's. It meant "comforter," and it suited him. This Nahman, however, was not a rebbe. He was not even the nominal head of the community; but on Friday nights, he was very simply its spiritual leader, the one who took us all into the comfort of the Sabbath through its sweet melodies.

In the United States I had often heard rabbis called "spiritual leaders." There the title was one of those arch phrases American Jews used to add luster to what they thought was the insufficiently distinguished title of "rabbi." In my memory it somehow never seemed to fit the people who held it, while here it was just right, for, as I would discover this evening, it was precisely the spirit that Nahman led.

I looked around for Menachem. We were about to usher in the Sabbath and I could find him nowhere in my line of sight. Where would he fit into this "show"? I wondered. But I couldn't find him, and my friend had never heard of him.

"Lechu nerannena"—Come, let us sing to the Lord— Nahman chanted the opening words of the Ninety-fifth Psalm with which the Sabbath service began. The sound jarred me out of my reverie and I looked at the cantor who led the service. He seemed to have become transformed. No longer aware of anyone around him, he closed his eyes and then opened them to focus off into the middle distance. I saw that he was seeing something that I could not myself see—at least, not yet. He clapped his hands together almost like a little boy, in ecstatic little motions. Held thus together, they were no longer open to take in the room; they were directed elsewhere.

The crowd too seemed to shift palpably, as if they knew that the Sabbath had now officially summoned from them some additional spirit. And it seemed to me suddenly that I had been wrong about many of the people around me. They were not, after all, like me, for they had somehow acquired the capacity to engage themselves in another world while I still stood where I had begun. I saw and felt the change around me, but still I hung back. It seemed somehow too easy, too artificial to change, even if I felt the attraction of the prayers. Changes were not supposed to take place that easily. Only amateurs believed in such magic transformation. Insiders like me knew better. Ecstasy couldn't happen on cue. I focused on the outsiders, those who put on rapturous displays or who shook their bodies just the wrong way. My observer's eye would keep me from being swept into something I was not ready to join.

The *neshama yetara*, that extra soul one is supposed to acquire on the Sabbath, was struggling to come out. Was that how Menachem would have explained what was happening to me? I thought for a moment about something I had once read somewhere about entities in this world which act upon us but which we do not recognize because we have never bothered to encounter them face to face. At times, they pass nearby and we turn the other way. I had had such experiences in my life. Sometimes they gave me a chill on the back of my neck; sometimes they made my stomach jump. I had learned to control them by avoiding them, by looking elsewhere. My talent for turning myself into an observer, one who would distance himself from the action, was, I supposed, a way to prevent myself from having to see or feel this sort of thing.

"The Lord is King."

I overheard the prayers somewhere underneath my thoughts.

"His lightnings illuminate the world; the earth beholds and trembles."

I was being led through some religious thicket by the sounds and words of the psalms. It had begun that evening I first met Menachem, and it was continuing still.

The best show in town, my friend had told me. But I hadn't realized that the audience and performers mingled on a single stage. I liked to sit in the back rows, staring out of the darkness at others in the light. But the house lights and those on stage were one and the same here.

"Light is sown for the righteous, and joy for the upright in heart," Nahman's voice penetrated my consciousness.

I was hearing in these prayers words I had not ever heard so clearly. Was it the inflections of Nahman's chanting or simply something inside me—the inner heart Menachem had spoken of—that was coming to life and beginning to echo sounds which until now had been flat? My friend had said that the singing here was *lebedik*. That meant "lively." Just an expression, I had assumed. But the life that the prayers were taking on, that had entered my reveries, was something wholly unexpected.

Nahman was beginning the *"Lecha dodi,"* the love poem which celebrates the mating of the Jews with their Sabbath. Written nearly half a millennium earlier, these were words with which Jews had for many generations greeted the Sabbath. But though I knew the lines by heart, the tunes accompanying them were new. And yet at the same time they were easy to sing. There was a sort of uncanny familiarity about them. Each stanza had its own melody, and as Nahman led us all in the singing, he seemed as well to lead us into some new level of consciousness, to some new religious pitch.

My reverie must have ended—or maybe the world around me had entered it. I was not at all sure. But I was face to face with the Sabbath in a way that I had never been before.

As a boy I had sometimes ushered in the Sabbath with my father as we sat at home and chanted these same prayers. At the last stanza, my father would stand and turn around, walk toward the door and bow low as he recited the closing words: "Come, O bride; come, O bride." The bride, of course, was the Sabbath, and we, the Jewish people, were her bridegroom. When I asked why he turned and bowed this way, he explained simply that we bridegrooms had to face our bride when she entered. So I had faced her and bowed too. But I had never seen her.

I always knew she had arrived. After all, the house was different; my parents had changed, and so had the rules of my world. The walls of the Law within which we lived seemed higher and more protective during the Sabbath. So there was never any mistaking her presence. And I had kept the Sabbath during all those years because I had learned to luxuriate in its presence and protection. I had learned how to lock out the pressures of mundane everydayness. But I had never seen the Sabbath face to face.

Tonight I could see her.

In the story of the giving of the Ten Commandments, the rabbis had been puzzled by the verse "And all the people *saw* the thunderings and the lightnings. . . ." How could they see sounds? Tonight I understood how people could see through sounds.

The people around me now looked different too. Nahman had peeled back their veneers to reveal another aspect. I had been wrong. They were not at all like me—at least, not now. Or maybe I wasn't who I thought I was.

"And the Lord God blessed the Seventh Day and made it holy."

"But how did He make it holy?" the rabbis asked. "He blessed it with the light of human faces," they answered, "for the light of men's faces all week is not like their light on the Sabbath."

It was true; I could see it. What I had seen upon entering was those weekday faces. Until the beginning of the Sabbath, I had observed the posturing and displays. But now the light was different, and I saw another world.

The prayers ended, and most people moved toward the door. Nahman took off his *talis* and slipped on his fur *shtreimel*. He seemed once again aware of the world of men, offering everyone he came near his hand and Sabbath greetings. A few people seemed to be coming in rather than leaving. I stood off at the side to watch.

The white shirts became fewer in number and the black and gold coats multiplied. Out of the lines of people a circle formed and began to make its way around the outside of the room, until it was complete and closed. Softly at first and then with their voices rising, the dancers began to sing: "Satisfy us with Your goodness and gladden our hearts with Your salvation; purify our hearts to serve You truly."

The song was the same one I had heard the Bratslaver Hasidim dance to the night before. But now the tune was different, the tempo slower. The circle grew ever larger. A few of the white shirts joined in. And then a small boy held out his hand and drew me in too.

"Grant that we keep, O Lord our God, in love and goodwill, Your holy Sabbath." The boy next to me sang out louder than the rest. And I joined him.

Another song, a kabbalistic poem, came next; and most of the white shirts were drifting away after two or three circuits of the room. But I stayed on, wondering if I would feel again the awe that I had experienced earlier. Around and around we went. The poem seemed to go on endlessly.

Through the open door I could see small groups of people standing outside and chatting, exchanging gossip and Sabbath greetings, while I went around and around with the Hasidim. Again the tune had changed, and so too the words. The words were unfamiliar. The verses we sang were extolling Reb Nahman of Bratslav. I could read them off one of the posters on the wall. They made an acrostic of the Rebbe's name.

I was not ready for this. The heights to which I had been earlier lifted were gone, and the indefinable presence of the Rebbe was instead bearing down on me. I felt increasingly uncomfortable, trapped, betrayed, as if I had been lured into this world under false pretenses. I had stayed too long.

Something like this had happened once before in my life with Hasidim. For years I had forgotten the experience, but now, as I felt pushed and pulled around the circle, the memory came back vividly, as if it were all happening again. The scene had taken place while I was at college. Three Hasidim had been invited by some Jewish campus organization to spend a weekend with the students. The thought of seeing these foreigners on campus had intrigued a number of us, and we went to hear the speakers on Friday night. Expecting some far-out calls for repentance or at the very least Buber's *Tales of the Hasidim* come to life, my friends and I were surprised to find an erudite and intelligent speaker who gave a reasoned talk about philosophy and religion —a talk not greatly different from what we might have heard in one of our classes.

As the Sabbath wore on, the Hasidim gradually wove more and more of a spell over us. They refused to fit our stereotypic expectations. After the speech they gathered around a long table and sang appealing melodies and then—in the style of Buber— finally did tell those stories we had been awaiting. Throughout, however, they never breathed a word or uttered a sound that seemed out of place in the university. The tunes were, after all, like folk tunes, and those were wildly popular then. The speeches were college lectures, and the stories were simply charming. Nothing was odd.

By the end of Sabbath, I was hooked. So when the visitors announced that they would organize a *melave malka*, the

Saturday-night celebration that marked the Jewish reluctance to allow the Sabbath "queen" to leave with anything less than a fanfare of song and story, I decided to change my plans for a movie and go instead to the anthropology museum where the party was to be held.

When I got there, I found that not everyone had been moved to come as I had. Only a few students were there. But to my surprise, dozens of Hasidim from the surrounding area had come to the campus to celebrate the *melave malka.* Permitted to drive, now that the Sabbath was over, they had come out in great numbers and seemed to surround me and my fellow students as we sat around a long table in the entrance hall of the museum.

Having thus locked us all in, they began to sing and tell stories about Hasidism, its beliefs and demands. But what we now heard no longer sounded as if it belonged on the campus. They excoriated those of us who had chosen this world over the demands of our faith. The speaker sounded more and more like an old-style preacher, berating those who sought salvation in the university and its false gods; and the songs he sang, along with his followers, seemed incantations meant to bring out in me another side of my personality. I was angry and disturbed. There was, I thought then, no difference between the primitives whose gods were in the museum cases around me and those whose rebbe had sent them on a mission to my college. I broke out of the circle and fled from the museum.

It was this feeling of being surrounded that came back to me now as I circled the room with the Bratslavers. I dropped my hands, and as I edged away from the Bratslav circle, I experienced again those feelings which had rooted themselves somewhere inside me. Outside the door, I began to wonder if indeed I had really seen the Sabbath face to face earlier, or had what I

had witnessed been a phantom, a mask under which the Rebbe
—and not the Sabbath—greeted me.

"Your father," I asked the little boy whom I recognized on
the steps: "where is he?"

"At the Kotel."

"But you told me yesterday that he comes home for the
Sabbath."

"He does."

"Then why is he at the Kotel?"

"Because that's where he receives the Sabbath," the boy answered, and skipped away.

Once again, I had been mistaken. Menachem came home on
the Sabbath, but not to the Bratslav synagogue. But now, I
wondered, was there any longer a point to meeting him at all?
Bratslav was not going to be the place where I would find my
chavruse, and maybe that was what Menachem had realized all
along and had sent me to find out for myself. Still, I wanted to
speak to him.

The next afternoon, in the waning hours of the Sabbath, I
decided to walk to the Kotel, hoping to find Menachem there. I
left with a single-minded determination, unable to think of anything other than how I would confront this strange man.

The walk from my apartment to the Wall normally took a
little over a half-hour. But it was a half-hour that always seemed
to bring about a subtle change in me, regardless of the mood
in which I started out.

I fairly ran down the hill toward the Yemin Moshe neighborhood, the little mews that had once been among the first Jewish
settlements outside the Old City walls but which had now
become a rich man's paradise of renovated old houses. The new
under cover of the old. At the bottom of steps on which the

houses were built I stood in the valley that had once been called Emek ha-Bacha—the ancient Vale of Tears.

Before me rose Mount Zion. "Beautiful in elevation, the joy of the whole earth is Mount Zion." The Psalms said that. And it was true. Mount Zion: my grandparents had dreamed of it— but never, I was told, did they ever imagine in those dreams that they would see it; and now I was about to climb it. To walk the mountain that for generations had symbolized all the yearnings of my people for a return to its former glories—I could never help becoming overwhelmed at the prospect of my ascent.

Going up was never easy. By the time I reached a halfway point on the hill, my shirt was wet all along my spine. At the top, where the winds from the valley below seemed to blow me further along, I always got a chill, perhaps intensified by the awe that I felt as I stared at the Old City walls on my right and then down into the Vale of Tears on my left and at the city beyond. "God in her palaces has made Himself known as a stronghold," the psalmist wrote. He must have been standing here as he composed those words.

"Walk about Zion, go round her, count her towers, mark well her ramparts, go through her palaces, that you may tell later generations . . ." he had added.

I turned in once again at Street of the Jews, past the ChaBaD house and on toward the Kotel. It was *mincha* time now, and the *lernen* had stopped while the *yeshiva* boys went to their prayers. From a few of the many small synagogues that dotted the Quarter I could already hear the *zemiros*, hymns that traditional Jews sang around the *Seuda Shlishis* table.

The custom of eating three feasts on the Sabbath is quite old. The first is Friday night, when Sabbath is first welcomed. The second comes after the morning prayers, when Jews return from the synagogue and in the leisure afforded by the day of rest, they sit around the table chanting poems and ballads that have made their way into the liturgy and the hearts of the people. But the third festive meal, the *Seuda Shlishis*, is always the most moving one, for it is eaten after the *mincha* and just before the Sabbath light fades away into the darkness. Even the tunes are different, often sung in minor keys and with a timbre that resonates with nostalgia and reluctance. Jews eat less at this meal than at the others, but they sing more. These were the songs I now heard as I passed along the narrow alleys on my way to the Kotel.

There were religious Jews who skipped the eating completely at that last meal. They were among those who believed that by the end of Sabbath, that day which the rabbis say gives us a taste of the everlasting world to come, people no longer need material sustenance. They need food for the heart and soul and not the stomach. So these Jews believe that *Seuda Shlishis* should be replaced by *lernen*, the true source of Sabbath nourishment. That was the sort of "Third Meal" I was going to have this evening. But as I walked toward the Kotel, I didn't yet know it.

The plaza in front of the Wall was largely empty as I made my way toward the men's section. A powerful breeze blew across the open space. In front of me, a tourist ran after his cardboard skullcap which had blown off. But this was not the sight that caught my eye.

In the corner, just where the divider separating the men's and women's sections of the space met the Wall, a man stood, his arms flailing wildly. In front of him were a hundred or more people who sat on benches or stood listening to him. And behind the divider, a few women pressed their ears against the cracks to hear. I moved closer.

He seemed to be reviewing the week's reading from the Torah. Here was another *maggid*. He looked nothing like the man I had heard at Shaarey Chesed. Young, slim, with a clipped beard, he wore no hat—only a plain blue skullcap. But it was not his appearance that seemed to be mesmerizing all those around him; it was the way he spoke. Possessed by the words, he jumped around as he spoke. He screamed; he cried and laughed. And always he flailed his arms about wildly. I stopped and listened.

"And Jacob our father went out from Beersheba and went toward Haran. And he stopped at a certain place, and spent the night there because the sun was beginning to set.

"Gentlemen, he prepared himself a place to lie down, and after he prayed, he began to dream. Oh, what a dream he had. Angels! Do you hear me? Angels. He saw angels—we don't see such angels ever, but our father Jacob was such a saint that he could see them going up and then coming down on a ladder that reached to heaven, to where the Holy One, blessed be He, stood. And the Master of the Universe spoke to our father Jacob and promised him, as it is written: 'The land upon which you rest I shall give to you and your children ever after. And you shall spread forth from it toward the sea in the west and toward the east, to the north and to the south.'

"Gentlemen, the Master of the Universe knew that a great people would come out of Jacob. And He knew that we could not exist without His blessing, so he added: 'I am with you and will guard you in all the places you go to and will bring you again into this land, for I shall not leave you until I have accomplished all that I have told you.'

"Our God will not leave us. You hear, our God will not leave us. We are His children, and He watches over us from the sea in the west to the Jordan in the east, to the Lebanon in the north and to Egypt in the south.

"You know the righteous Rabbi Mendel of Viznitz, may his memory be a blessing, told a story about a Hasid who once came to the sainted Rabbi Levi Yitzhak of Berditchev and complained to him that his circumstances were very bad, that he owed a great deal of money, but the world did not yet know it, thinking him still a rich man. And now through a series of bad dealings he had lost all his money. Oh, we know how easily that can happen."

A chuckle ran through the crowd. I sat down.

"And now he had lost all his money, but not a living soul knew of his fate.

"So the rabbi suggested that he buy a lottery ticket and with the help of God he might be saved from ruin."

A few people laughed. Didn't they buy such tickets all the time—but who ever won?

"But the Hasid was worried lest the help not come in time. You would worry too.

"After all, he thought, sometimes it takes years to win, and in the meantime my creditors are at the door, and I have a daughter who needs to be married off.

"Rabbi Levi Yitzhak assured the Hasid that the Lord, may He be blessed, would bring the money in good time.

"Of course, the Hasid followed the advice of the *zaddik* and bought a lottery ticket. On his way home he stopped at an inn, and there he planned to spend the night. That evening, an important officer also stopped at that very same inn. Oh! God works His miracles in the most mysterious ways. The officer too decided to spend the night there.

"That night the officer had a dream that in that inn there was a Jew who had a lucky lottery ticket, and that he should exchange his own ticket for the Jew's, for the Jew's would surely be a winner while his own was worth nothing.

"And the officer awoke and realized that it was all a dream. But when he fell back asleep he had the same dream again. So when he awoke again, he asked his aide to investigate whether or not such a Jew with a lottery ticket was truly at the inn. His aide went and found the Jew and brought him before the officer.

" 'Do you have a lottery ticket?' the officer asked the Jew.

" 'Yes,' he answered.

" 'So do I. Come let us exchange tickets, and I will add some pieces of gold to your price.'

"But the Jew refused the offer and said: 'Even should you give me a great sum of gold, I would not part with this ticket.'

"The officer persisted, raising the price of his offer until it stood at a thousand gold pieces. But the Jew steadfastly refused."

The people around me leaned forward in their seats. The *maggid* rocked toward his audience. More persons wandered over to listen. I had forgotten Menachem completely.

"The officer got up in anger and commanded his aide to take the ticket from the Jew with force. And thus the aide did, grabbing the Jew and wresting from him the ticket, and he gave it to his officer.

"Now the officer said to the Jew: 'Still and all, I do not want to rob you, so here—take the thousand gold pieces that I offered you and my lottery ticket as well.'

"Against his will, the Hasid took the money and the new ticket and replied: *'Gam zu le tovah'* [This too shall be for good]. What faith, gentlemen! Would we have stood the test?

"So, my friends, the Jew traveled home and, using some of the gold pieces, he married off his daughter with a great wedding.

"He returned to Berditchev and his rebbe. The *zaddik* said to him: 'I have seen that your fortune has dropped into the dust, and I forced those who control dreams to enter into the heart of that officer you met at the inn so that he would exchange tickets with you, for I saw that his ticket would win and yours would not. And the thousand gold pieces that he added into the bargain were there because you told me you had to marry off your daughter. So in the beginning you have had a small salvation and later your salvation shall be great.'

"The Hasid went home and became even richer than before.

"When the rabbi of Viznitz finished this story, he said: 'This is what the Holy One, blessed be He, meant when he promised our father Jacob: "I shall not leave you until I have accomplished all that I have told you." For now we have had small salvations, little victories. But the great salvation is yet to come. And our God, may He be blessed, will not leave us until He has brought it to us.'"

"True and certain," I heard someone near me say.

An old man sitting next to me turned and said, "A day before our soldiers captured the Kotel, no one even dreamed this was possible. The victory came suddenly and unexpectedly. Is it not true?"

I nodded.

"That's a sign," he added, "a sign that the Messiah will come suddenly, even though we don't expect him. For we have had small salvations, but the great salvation is yet to come." He patted me on the shoulder and walked away.

It was dark now, and someone to my left began to sing the psalm that marks the beginning of the end of the Sabbath. He closed his eyes and held a finger near his ear, seeming to shut out everything but his song. I found the page and sang along for a few verses.

Again I had become caught in a religious thicket and had missed Menachem. Determined to find him, I crossed the plaza and walked toward one of the arches inside which a small light burned. A small group of men were still huddled there around a table, reviewing the Mishna Brura, the same code of Jewish law I had been studying afternoons at Shaarey Chesed.

I couldn't hear them from where I stood in the shadows and therefore moved closer. The light shone across my face. With the end of the Sabbath, the class was ending. Some of the men had already shut their books; they sat and listened to the teacher's last words. I still couldn't hear him, but it was too late now, for like everyone else, these men too were about to begin the *ma'ariv* prayers to close the Sabbath.

I walked toward the corner where I had seen Menachem that first day. But a service was just beginning there, and I could see only a small mass of people huddled together reciting the prayers.

Like a wave, the first few words of the *ma'ariv* passed across the plaza. "Bless the Lord, Who is blessed."

I stopped now to join one group. Someone handed me a prayer book, and I like the others around me plunged into the prayers. "The great salvation is yet to come." The words still hung in my memory.

"*Shavua tov*"—a good week—people greeted one another with the end of the service.

I was reluctant to go without finding Menachem. Near the gate, a group of Jews had gathered to recite the *havdala*, the separation ceremony with which the Sabbath would be put away until next week. Someone distributed myrtle branches; someone else gave out sprigs of thyme. We would take in their aroma when it came time to make the blessing over sweet smells. A large twisted candle was lit. I could not see the flame, but the light shone out from somewhere inside the group of people in front of me, so that what I could see was the glow of their faces.

"Behold, the Lord is my salvation; I will trust and will not be afraid." The *havdala* had begun. And then the voice came to that point in the ceremony where we were all supposed to respond: "The Jews had light and joy, gladness and honor. So be it with us."

Behind me I heard a voice echo these words. I wheeled around to look. It was Menachem.

SIX

At the Crossroads

Only a few days had passed since I had first met Menachem Reichler, but as I stood at the *havdala* ceremony in the afterglow of the Sabbath, I felt as if that meeting had taken place somewhere far in the past. Perhaps it was because I had been living with the thought of him almost incessantly since that time. Twice I had been attracted and then repelled by the Hasidic world from which he came. Now, once again, I felt the attraction.

The *havdala* ceremony ended, and the candle was extinguished. The air was sweet with the smell of the myrtle and thyme over which people had made the ritual blessing for a sweet week and which they still held in their hands. There was laughter, as one by one men offered one another good wishes for the upcoming week and then started on their ways home. Behind me, Menachem Reichler had already begun his departure, and I hurried after him toward the stairs that led back to his cubicle in the Jewish Quarter.

"Mr. Reichler?"

He seemed not to hear me and kept walking.

I called louder, but still the man in front of me failed to respond.

I was nearly next to him when I realized that the person I had been following was not Menachem Reichler. In the darkness, I had apparently confused him with another of the Hasidim in the crowd. Indeed, there was no one ahead of me who even remotely resembled the man I was looking for, so I retraced my steps toward the Kotel. But now I was beginning to wonder whether or not I had really seen Reichler earlier. After all, it had been dark, and I had perhaps been a little too eager to find him by then. Besides, I had only once in my life seen the man, and although I believed that I knew exactly what he looked like, I might be mistaken. It would not be the first time in the last few days that the relationship between my perceptions and reality had become confused.

As I neared the Wall, I could hear some singing coming from inside the arches on the side. That was where the Bratslavers normally greeted the Sabbath. Perhaps they were ushering her out there as well. Saturday night was, after all, the time for *melave malka*, and Hasidim were always reluctant to let Sabbath slip away quietly and without notice.

I had guessed right. About ten men had formed a circle inside the first archway, and there they were dancing around and around as they sang a variety of songs that celebrated the special ties between the Jewish people and their holy Sabbath. They seemed to gather speed with each chorus they sang.

And then suddenly there was silence. The little circle disintegrated and the men each turned toward the Wall, many of them pressing their bodies and faces against it while murmuring a prayer. I picked up and opened a prayer book.

"Master of All Worlds, Father of Mercy and Forgiveness, under a good sign and a good star, allow the six days of activity about to begin to be passed in peace, protected from all sin and transgression, unblemished by wrongdoing, misconduct or guilt; days during which we cleave to the study of Your Torah and to righteous ways."

It was a prayer I could recite in good conscience.

As fast as their dance had been, so, in contrast, were these prayers recited slowly. But even after my habituation in slow prayer at Shaarey Chesed, I still had not disciplined my spirit to move slowly enough for these Hasidim, and so I finished before most of those around me. Looking about, I saw Menachem standing in the corner, one foot in front of the other, as he had been when I had first seen him. This time I resolved not to take my eyes off him until I had spoken to him.

Back and forth he swayed, holding the prayer book close to his chest. He knew the prayer by heart, but seemed nevertheless to want to hold the words near his heart. When he had finished he closed the book, folded it against himself and kissed the stone in front of his face. It was a tiny motion, but he managed to do it all in a single movement that made me think for a moment he had fainted and fallen against the Wall.

He turned toward the exit, and I tried frantically to catch him with my eyes. But although he looked in my direction, he seemed not to see me.

"Mr. Reichler?"

He looked up but did not appear to recognize me.

"I spoke with you one day last week. Your father sent me to you for help in finding a *chavruse*. Do you remember?"

He smiled and started walking again. "Come."

I followed him up the stairs. In minutes we were sitting in his room, and he was lighting the kerosene stove. It cast a giant shadow of him against the wall. Because his back was to me, I looked at the shadow while I spoke.

"You told me that I should go to the Bratslav *bes medresh* in

Katamonim and there you would show me how to discover my own way to *lernen*. But when I went you were not there."

"Did you discover anything?" he asked.

"I discovered that I could not be a Bratslaver Hasid."

"And did you discover what you could be?"

"I was hoping you would help me do that."

"And how do you think I could do that?" For the first time tonight, he turned toward me and looked straight into my eyes as he spoke.

"You came searching for a *chavruse*. Does this not mean that you are ready to *lern*, to plunge yourself into the fires of Torah and to let them fire the faith in your heart of hearts?"

His figures of speech set the pattern for mine. I had to speak in images I thought he could understand and accept.

"But you told me that only if I discovered the character of my heart of hearts would I be able to find the proper teacher."

"And did I say I would do that for you? Did I not tell you that you had to take in the burning coals of Torah in order to purify yourself? Did you do that?"

"I tried."

"What does this mean, 'I tried'?"

"I wanted very much to join in what I saw, but I felt that I didn't belong there. I tried twice. And twice I failed. The first night I studied with the *chavruse* in the *bes medresh*. But I could not immerse myself in the teachings of Hasidism; I could not persuade myself of the importance of what the Rebbe had written. I felt uncomfortable, inauthentic. I thought perhaps you had sent me to discover that, to realize that I had to find my own place, one different from yours. Still, I wanted to be sure. So when your son told me you came back to Katamonim for Shabbos, I went back last night to find you."

"*Nu?*" he asked, prompting me to continue.

"So at first it was wonderful. The singing lifted me and made me feel the entrance of Shabbos in a completely new way. But in the end, when I once again entered the circle, I felt that I did not belong."

"What does this mean, that you felt you did not belong?"

"I am not a Bratslaver Hasid. I do not accept the power of the Rebbe's teaching. I cannot sing praises to his memory because it doesn't live in me. And I do not want to bring it into me. I simply want to have the experience of *lernen* as I told you."

For a moment it seemed that there was a faint smile on Menachem's face, as if he had heard something he had been waiting to hear. I turned my head for a moment, and when I looked back he had once again taken on the intent gaze that seemed to look through my eyes.

"I have spent time *lernen* with a *chavruse* at Shaarey Chesed. For months, I went each night to review *Gemara* with a wonderful group of men who loved the pages they studied and who let me into their circle, but in the end I felt that I did not really belong there either. There they studied only those tractates dealing with the sacrifices, and I just don't have the capacity to become caught up in a discussion of such things. For a time I tried, and I felt a real closeness to the men with whom I *lernt*. But in the end, I left."

Menachem looked at me without speaking for what seemed an eternity. Then, finally, in a soft but firm voice, he spoke: "Late one night a blind man was about to go home after visiting a friend. 'Please,' he said to his friend, 'may I take your lantern with me?'

" 'Why carry a lantern?' asked his friend. 'You won't see any better with it.'

" 'No,' said the blind man, 'maybe not. But others will see me better and not bump into me.'

"So his friend gave the blind man the lantern, inside which was a candle.

"The blind man had not gone more than a few meters into the darkness when someone walked right into him. The blind man was very angry and cried out: 'Why don't you look out? Why don't you see this lantern?'

"'Why don't you light the candle?' asked the other."

Menachem paused and then continued, his voice louder this time.

"You know, a young man once came to the Rizhyner Rebbe, may his memory be a blessing, and told him: 'During the hours when I devote myself to my studies, I feel life and light, but the moment I stop studying it is all gone. What should I do?'

"And the Rebbe replied: 'That is just as when a man walks through the woods on a dark night, and for a time another joins him, lantern in hand, but at the crossroads they part and the first must grope his way on alone. But if a man carries his own light with him, he need not be afraid of any darkness.' Do you understand? It is time for you to stop looking for someone else to lead you, for someone else's lantern. You must at last learn to study on your own."

Menachem walked out of the room for a moment. I thought about what he had said.

The men of the study circle in Shaarey Chesed; Abraham Krol; Yosef Moshe Reichler; his son Menachem and the Bratslaver Hasidim had each joined me for a time with their lanterns. At first the brightness they brought into my life had been awe-inspiring—even blinding. But in each case, as I grew accustomed to their light, I had seen that those who held the lanterns were coming from and going to a path I could not follow. And in the end, I had left each, to grope on alone.

But unlike the man in the Rizhyner rabbi's story, I did not return at the crossroads to the same darkness from which I had entered the pathway of *lernen*. Even after I stopped attending regularly, my place at Shaarey Chesed had been saved, and I sometimes returned to it. On Friday evenings, I would continue to welcome the Sabbath at Bratslav—although I could no longer stay for the Rebbe's dance. These afterglows remained, but I still had not emerged with my own light in hand.

Menachem came back inside. He held a book in his hand.

"Do you remember what Rabbi Yossi tells us in *Avot?*"

Menachem pointed to the open page in his hand. "He says: 'Repair yourself to study Torah.' What does this mean?" Menachem paused. He let the question reverberate in the silence of his room. I did not try to answer, and he continued. "Rashi tells us that it means that a man cannot become a scholar on the merit of his father's studies but has to repair and prepare himself to study on his own. And the Rambam adds that without such repair, even the greatest intelligence is worthless."

He closed the book carefully, kissed it and placed it on the table nearby. We were both silent now. He walked to the Primus and turned it off.

"Repair to your room and be alone with yourself. Come out when you are ready. That is what I have been trying to do myself here. Only you can do it for yourself; I cannot help you any further."

There was a calm determination in his voice that left no room for further questions or debate. He was right. I had to decide for myself what I was really looking for and what I was prepared to study.

SEVEN

Repair

A PERSON can spend time with himself on the streets as easily
as and sometimes more easily than in his room. For the
next few days, I walked the streets of Jerusalem. Not the Old
City—that was too filled with sights and sounds that would take
me away from myself. I went instead to the neighborhoods
adjacent to Mea Shearim. Here where every other doorway
seemed to lead to a synagogue or study room, I thought I might
find a place for myself. Here was the world where people remained attached to an eternal landscape of the past and to the
tradition. And here, I believed, I might discover whether or not
I still had any connection to that world.

Every so often I would walk into one or another little synagogue, directing my feet with a studied determination toward
the corner or bench where men sat at study and resolved that I,
like them, would take down a volume from the shelf and begin
to *lern* on my own in their company. But when I got inside, all I
discovered was my feelings of embarrassment and a sense of
being out of place. And so I would act as if I had forgotten
something, turn and leave. The anxieties I harbored toward this

world seemed to be getting the better of me. The harder I tried to find a way in, the harder it seemed to be to stay once I got inside.

Back on the street, I caught the bus pulling up at the corner. It was bus number nine. Of all the lines running through the city, none offers a more remarkable route than number nine. Starting from the central bus station and its social underlife, it winds its way through the posh neighborhood of Rehavia, populated by government officials and wealthy Ashkenazim, past the headquarters of the Chief Rabbinate, fancy tourist hotels and the Jewish Agency building where the modern Zionist state was born. From there the bus continues into the city center, where it skirts the open-air vegetable market filled with bargain hunters on one side and on the other the golden triangle of streets named Ben Yehuda, King George and Jaffa with their expensive specialty shops and department stores. Next it turns up a hill past the old Bikur Cholim hospital, touches the fringes of Mea Shearim and then drives past the massive houses and up the wide avenues of the once grand Bukharian quarter, built in the nineteenth century by rich Jews from Bukhara, in central Asia; it was here, they believed, that their great salvation would someday come as the Messiah, on his way from the Mount of Olives on the other side of the valley, stopped to rest in their sumptuous homes.

Afterward, number nine glides across the old border that cut the city in half before the 1967 war and passes from old salvations to new ones, alongside the symmetrical, gleamingly modern apartment blocks and little shopping centers of Ramat Eshkol. Finally, the end of the line and the bus climbs up to Mount Scopus.

A ride on number nine from beginning to end is a trip across every kind of border, through various circles of Jewish existence, back and forth from old to new. In each neighborhood the people getting on and off the bus change. And if one allows himself to become imaginatively transformed with each turn— to become, as I did on occasion, a part of what he observes— the ride can be a sort of spiritual journey through Jewish life. Today I had joined the tour in the precincts of Orthodoxy and allowed myself to be taken away to another domain.

As I sat on the bus, I thought how much the ride served as a metaphor for what I had been through. I too had skirted Mea Shearim and touched its fringes, and then had made my way to modern times. And like the old folks of Bukhara, I also waited for the great salvation that was to come—although just what sort of salvation would save the likes of me I did not really know.

Mount Scopus, the end of the line. To the east, where rain never falls, lies the awesome wilderness of Judea. The prophet Jeremiah, and others like him, had always found a needed solitude there when the city and its people became too much. To the west lay Jewish civilization. Scopus, "the place of beholding": from this mountain, pilgrims approaching Jerusalem first glimpsed the Holy Temple atop nearby Moriah. Here was the last place the Roman general Titus had camped before he marched upon Jerusalem. Perhaps it was here that Yochanan ben Zakkai had met with Vespasian and struck his bargain for Yavneh. From here generations of Jews had looked out upon the destruction their holy city had become. From here came Jewish memories, and here some hopes were spawned.

But Scopus was now something else. Since April 1925, the Hebrew University had stood here. Enlarged after 1967 when the ground around it was regained, the place now hugged the mountain like a fortress. Here, perhaps more than anywhere else in the city, I felt at home and strangely safe. Here, like the bus, I came to rest and for repair. This was, after all, the university—and that was where I best fitted in, where I had already learned how to learn and where I knew I should at last return.

I walked to the library and found the social-science section. In the past, whenever I felt overwhelmed by the people and places I observed, I had often been able to steady myself by walking amid the stacks and pulling down one work or another of anthropology. The walls of books around me seemed a sort of protective shelter in which I would find my way. The content of the books could help as well. To learn how others had navigated their way through the worlds and ways of life they studied had always helped me find my bearings. But as I wandered between the shelves of books and scanned the titles before my eyes, I realized that this time the library would not steady me.

These books mainly told one how to deal with "going native"; but what I had always feared might happen had now begun to happen: I was "going stranger." My journey to Jerusalem in the footsteps of Yochanan ben Zakkai, I had believed, would enable me to share in an experience that had always remained on the periphery of my life. I had not, however, expected to be swallowed up by it completely—to become only a participant; but neither had I supposed I would have to escape to the distance of being purely an observer. Yet now I could neither find my way in, nor could I any longer tolerate being outside.

The world of *lernen* into which I had wandered had worked its charms upon me. I was touched by it; and then that touch frightened me, because I knew that however much I tried to identify with the traditional Jews around me, I would never give up who I was, abandon my foothold in the modern world in favor of their world. I might study the Torah again and again, but did I really believe now that everything was contained in it? Was I ready to grow old and gray over it? Would I never swerve from it? Certainly not. I was still a professor of sociology.

Yet precisely because I had been with the men in the study circle, around the pages of holy books, in ways that I had never been before; because I felt, when I was with them, that I was still very deeply bound to the Orthodox world, I also realized that I could never be satisfied living outside the boundaries of their domain. If, before these experiences, I had been an outsider to *lernen*, now I felt more like an expatriate.

Something beyond the social scientist in me had been affected in Jerusalem. It was not my professional technique or methods that needed repair; it was something in me, something I needed to find that would open me and the world of *lernen* to each other without forcing me to change myself. I would not ever become a Bratslaver Hasid or one of those men of Shaarey Chesed. I would not replace earthly Jerusalem with its heavenly counterpart. But, surely, I was more than just a sociologist.

Slowly and almost unconsciously, I left the library and made my way to the southern tip of the campus, far from the classrooms and the books, to a place where people seldom came, and found myself a plot of grass where at last, alone, I came to clear my thoughts and chart my forward motion. From here I could see both sides of the mountain.

What really had attracted me to the world of the Reichlers, Rav Krol, Mintzer the book dealer, Bratslav and the others? Why had I been able for a time to feel so comfortable there?

Perhaps those voices from the holy books of my people which I had heard as a boy in my background, and which as a "college graduate" I had tried to still, were now once again echoing in the inner chambers of my consciousness. The content of the Talmud might even now not always please me or be completely comprehensible, its turns of logic often too complex or apparently archaic for me to appreciate; but its cadences and rhythms, its phrases and idioms embedded in rabbinic dialogue and debate contained something of the voice of my people and the soul of its wisdom.

But there was more. I had seen and heard people *lernen* who

could engage in eternal debates and visualize ancient ceremonies with all the freshness of a first-time experience. For
them, but not for me, the descriptions in the Talmud of the High
Priest's activities at the Holy Temple were reminiscences of
something they seemed to have witnessed. They walked with
him into the courtyard of the Temple, watched him as he put on
all his vestments, traced the arc of his arm as he sprinkled the
blood of his sacrifice upon the altar. Then, just as easily, they
became the ancient rabbis who argued over exactly how these
acts were performed. One saw it one way, the other another.

The men of Shaarey Chesed, the Hasidim of Bratslav could
move to other Jewish times and places through the pages of
their holy Jewish books. Now—as never before—I envied them
their capacities for transformation. And even though I could
not go with them and my intellect was often not engaged by the
words themselves, as I watched their eyes and listened to their
voices I sometimes felt uncannily at home, sustained by an attachment far deeper than anything I could fathom. Perhaps that
was why I sometimes felt as if I were part of something genuine
and pure whenever I came near the men who *lernt*.

That feeling had come and gone, and both the coming and
the going disturbed me in different ways. When I had become
attached to Bratslav and the world of *lernen*, I had in the end
felt myself robbed of my modernity. But when at last I became
estranged from the *bes medresh*, I also felt a sense of loss. I felt
that I had left the roots of my Jewish being. That second loss
was something new to me, and it forced me once again to reflect
on the nature of my ties to tradition.

Sitting here at the edge of the university—beyond the borders
of Mea Shearim and Bratslav—I had to admit to myself that I
remained, after all, an observant Jew, tied by inertia and
residual feelings of attachment to a way of life I could not,

would not leave. I could not allow myself to "go stranger." Too much of my personal history was still tied up in Judaism for me to abandon it all in favor of dispassionate, objective observations. The prayers, I had been told, of a miracle rabbi had cured my grandmother of her childhood blindness. My mother's father, a Hasid, had throughout life steeped himself in Torah study. My parents had survived the fire storm of Nazi persecution and the ashes of the concentration camps through what they said was their faith in God. When I was born (that birth itself their vote of confidence in God and life), my father had vowed that he would from then on never let a day pass without prayer—and till this day has kept that pledge. And still each night my mother lies in bed reciting psalms of thanksgiving and of praise; while mornings never pass without her special prayers for our family's welfare and future hopes. My wife and I had built a Jewish home; our children saw themselves thus strictly bound. Throughout my years while growing up, and now still, the house in which I felt at home reflected all this Jewish faith.

If in college and later, as I made my way into the outside world, acquired new perspectives and found myself an occupation, I tried at times to place my Judaism in private regions, I still had never removed it from my life. I lived an Orthodox life: prayed, kept the Sabbath, ate only kosher food and performed as many *mitzvos* as I could—even as I proceeded in the university and my profession. The back-and-forth rhythm that carried me between my two worlds had—because of my experiences in the study circle—been broken. Once again, I had to temper the tradition with my other life. That was the repair I genuinely needed.

I'd touched some worlds and they'd touched me, and was all that would be left of that my objectivity? What had started—so I thought—as research couched in Jewish terms had now become confused; and once again, as at the first, I had to decide what I was looking for and what sort of study I could pursue.

My wife knew little if anything of my growing confusion. I had abandoned her and my children for many hours as I made my way into the all-male world of the study circle. Although she had encouraged me at the beginning and had long ago learned to tolerate my anthropological travels, I knew that by now she quietly resented my long absences and her exclusion. But she had swallowed those feelings—perhaps as Menachem's wife must have done when her husband escaped to his room in the Old City. Sometimes, when I would be rushing off to *lern* instead of being with the children or sitting down to share some time with her, she would say, "I wish you didn't have to go."

And if I replied, "I'll stay if you like," she would answer, "No, you have to go; I want you to go. It's your responsibility as a Jew and a father to spend time studying."

How could I now tell her that the result of this effort was my estrangement from the very world she had painfully encouraged me to enter? Neither of us wanted that.

But was I really estranged from *lernen*? And did I want to "go native"? Was I still on a researcher's quest? Nothing was very clear. While I had leafed through a few pages of Talmud and watched as others made their way across the page, while I had seen the charm in what they did and been moved by it, I sat here now on the mountaintop still without a book and all alone.

When I'd embarked upon this trip, I'd felt the need to *lern*, but only as a distant voice from somewhere in my Jewish past. I had no sense of disrepair. Now that had changed. Perhaps that was why I had come at last to where I sat atop the watershed: against my back the university, to my right Jerusalem and on my left an endless wilderness. Somewhere among all this, there was direction—but where it was I did not know.

The sun was dropping past the domed rooftops, and the

winds of night rose up from the east. A chill upon my neck, I stood and turned toward the city, my questions unresolved but resolute in my intention to find my book and group and way.

My time in Jerusalem was not always taken up with spiritual matters. Among the mundane realities of my life was the endless need to exchange my dollars for Israeli shekels. Like other foreigners, therefore, I always seemed to be heading for the foreign-currency window at the bank. A creature of habit, I normally went to the bank closest to my apartment. Ian, the teller there, was pleasant and quick, qualities I'd often found missing at other banks. After two or three visits he began to recognize me, which meant that everything would go faster. He became for me yet another familiar face in this strange city, and I began to half–look forward to my visits to the bank. Like me, Ian was in his thirties, wore a knitted skullcap and was a native English speaker. During the several times a week I came into the bank, we would carry on a brief conversation—more than pleasantries but nothing of much consequence: just enough to allow for a feeling of camaraderie to grow between us.

Today, as he counted out my change, he looked up and remarked: "You know, I've never asked you what brought you to Jerusalem."

I mumbled something about *lernen*.

"Oh, you want to go to a *yeshiva*."

No, I explained, I wasn't really interested in reviewing Torah in the rarefied atmosphere of the *yeshiva*. The intensity and insularity of that life was too much for me. Instead, I wanted to join with Jews like him who review texts in the flow of their normal lives.

"You mean the people in the *bes medresh*?" he asked.

"Exactly."

"Well, I have a place for you." His eyebrows bobbed as he spoke. "You'll feel right at home."

"Where?"

"Right around the corner. I *daven* there. Why don't you come Tuesday night to our regular class? You'll see what I mean."

The line of people waiting for money was getting longer, but their patience was not. This was not a time to ask for details.

"Where do you live?" Ian asked. I told him.

"Meet me in front of your house at a quarter to eight Tuesday night. I'll take you there."

"You won't forget?"

"Don't worry. Just don't you forget to be there, because the rabbi likes to start on time."

I left the bank with a sense of excitement. Ian was like me—a modern man—and I was going to *lern* with him. This was not going to be another excursion into distant worlds. Perhaps at last I might be on my way.

On Tuesday evening I stood on the street in front of my apartment, waiting for my friend. He arrived on time, and I squeezed into his tiny Fiat, the sort that looks as if it could make a U-turn in a phone booth. We drove no more than five minutes before we got to a synagogue called Heichal Baruch—the sanctuary of Baruch.

"The building we're going to," Ian explained, pointing to the little alley ahead of us into which we walked, "used to be a British officers' hut during the period of the Mandate. In 1948, Shlomo—you'll meet him in a minute—led a battalion that took over control of it. After the war, he persuaded the government to let him make the hut into a synagogue. Since then, he's made it into his own *shtibble* and named it after his father. On Shab-

bos, he does everything: leads the prayers, reads from the Torah
—the works. He's the one who came to Rabbi Rotenbush—
that's our teacher—and asked him to give a class here once a
week."

Heichal Baruch was in a place I would never have found on
my own. Ian led me down a narrow alley behind a car-rental
office and under an archway atop which generations of pigeons
had roosted. The pavement crackled under our feet as we
walked among the encrusted droppings. An unfrosted light bulb
barely illuminated the path.

The sight was less than inviting, and as I walked up the two
steps that led to a nondescript gray door, I began to wonder if I
was heading again into another of those little backwater synagogues filled with black hats and coats. Would this be simply
another outpost of the world of Mea Shearim? But there was no
time to dwell on the question, for in a moment we were inside.

The light was blinding. Never had I seen so many lamps in
such a small room. Two large chandeliers with about fifteen
bulbs in each hung from the ceiling. Between them were rows of
fluorescent lights. On the walls there were little lamps that
beamed light into the corners, and in those corners were
memorial tablets in which some tiny bulbs burned in memory of
the dead. The Ark, a combination of wood and rather ugly
laminated plastic, was topped with a blue shield painted to look
like the heavens and studded with dozens of little electric flames
which when lit were apparently supposed to look like stars. To
its left and over the cantor's small pulpit was a seven-branched
menorah which burned brightly, and below it, encased in glass
and in front of a large amulet in the shape of a *menorah* on
which kabbalistic incantations were written, was a glass candelabrum which also could be lit. I could not count them, but
there seemed to be at least a hundred and fifty lamps of one sort
or another burning.

Yet for all its luminescence, the room was far from dazzling. The light illuminated utter plainness. A few handwritten verses from Jewish sources extolling the merits of prayer and study hung on one wall, bookcases were on another and hat racks were everywhere. Around the outer edges of the room were long, plain white plastic-topped tables which worshipers used for prayer, study or eating. In the middle was the table and pulpit from which the Torah was read. A worn red velour coverlet lay on top of it, its memorial inscription hardly legible any longer. A smaller room, separated from this one by a wall in which two windows had been cut, served—I later learned—as the women's section during prayers and also as the kitchen, social hall and community center.

The harshness of the light and the utter modesty of the furnishings contrasted so with the gloom in the alley that the total impression made by Heichal Baruch was of a sort of warm homeliness.

When we entered, most of the men were already seated around the table. Many of them looked like Ian or me. Dressed like inhabitants of the twentieth century, they reminded me of men among whom I had grown up in my modern Orthodox world. Still, after my experiences at Bratslav, I jumped to no conclusions about appearances. If I had learned nothing else from my wanderings in synagogues, I had learned that people could, once inside, acquire a new face and change their character.

A man of my father's age was handing out the volumes of Talmud. Short, somewhat chubby, baldingly gray, he smiled broadly and seemed the incarnation of a sweet Jewish old man —the kind who gives out candy to little children in the synagogue (which, it turned out, he did). Ian greeted him warmly as we entered and introduced me. Later he told me that this man —"Reb Shimileh"—was a refugee from Poland who had come to Israel just before the War of Independence. Somehow in all those years he had never managed to learn to speak Hebrew; he could understand it, but felt more at ease in Yiddish. Reb Shimileh had not been a religious Jew before the war. A bit of a socialist and a freethinker, he had been transformed by the experience of surviving two wars in such a short time. Escaping from the Nazis, who had murdered his wife and daughter, he came to Israel and was smuggled into Jerusalem. Here, during the siege of the city, he met his second wife, an Orthodox woman and war widow, whose daughter he had adopted. Now he had built a new life, one bounded by religion. But because he had never received a Jewish education, he was limited to "serving scholars," as he put it.

"In the place of the repentant, even the most righteous cannot stand," Ian explained, repeating the wisdom of the Talmud.

We walked in and I was introduced simply: "This is my friend Shmulik." He used the diminutive of my Hebrew name. "He's going to *lern* with us."

"*Baruch ha-Shem*"—Praised be God—Reb Shimileh answered. He patted me on the back and handed me a volume of the Talmud.

A few of the other men turned to nod or wave greetings. Shlomo, a dark, balding man with a pencil-thin mustache, sat at the front, next to where the rabbi—the "rav," the men called him—would sit. He held out his hand and shook mine. "There's always room for someone who wants to *lern* Torah."

There were about fifteen men present this evening. Later I would learn that they included bank tellers and managers, a schoolteacher, an official at the Ministry of Religion, a couple of shopkeepers, a metalworker and a wood turner, lab technicians, a chemist. But these roles in the world outside this room played hardly any part inside the borders of the study circle. Here new identities would be forged: scholar, riddler, joker and simpleton, the one who cued the teacher and the one who echoed him, those who led us off on tangents and those who brought us back to the text, those who could quote Scripture and those who could preempt the Talmud's questions. These were the identities that counted in this room.

I settled down next to Ian at the corner of the table and opened my book to the proper page. Since every edition of the Talmud is paginated in exactly the same way, I had no problem finding the place; a quick glance at my neighbor's pointing finger was all it took to get oriented.

A moment later the rav walked in; and following Shlomo's lead, we all stood. He was a tall man, dressed in rabbinic black. But there was a regal quality to his appearance. The hat he wore was a homburg, and his long waistcoat was impeccably pressed. His white shirt with its starched collar looked spotless. And unlike Hasidim, who, although they wore black hats and coats, never wore a tie, Rabbi Rotenbush had one on. But when he sat down, he seemed to doff the trappings of his rabbinic royalty and visibly relaxed. At first his hat came off, replaced by a big velvet skullcap. Next, he unbuttoned his coat and loosened his tie. He smiled and looked around at each of us, stopping at my stranger's face a bit longer than the others.

"A guest?" he asked.

"He wants to see how we *lern* here in Jerusalem," Ian explained before I could open my mouth.

"From abroad?"

"From America," I replied, wondering what there was about my appearance that gave away my origins.

"You have come to live here?"

I supposed by "here" he meant Jerusalem. But in a way I knew he meant as well to ask me if I had come to dwell within the fellowship of the *chavruse* or was I simply there to observe it once and leave. It was not a question I was ready to answer. But

I believed that if I ruled out the possibility completely, I could never be fully embraced by those in the circle. Could one take in a person who had already decided to remain a stranger? And I was not prepared to remain a stranger.

"Not yet," I replied.

A few of the men smiled along with the rav. My answer was ambiguous and open; there was hope in it—and there was a challenge here too, for perhaps it was up to them to hasten my decision by either bringing me in or leaving me out.

The rav looked away from me and seemed to address the others, but the message was directed straight at my heart.

"You know, gentlemen, in *Avot*, Rabbi Yosé ben Kisma tells a story."

Although I had not thought of it for years, I knew this Talmudic story well, for I had heard my father review it many times in my life. During the long summer Sabbath afternoons, as we sat around the dining-room table waiting for nightfall and the new week, the chapters of this book were often read aloud in my parents' house; and this one had been a favorite. But I said nothing, while the rav continued.

"He was once traveling on the road when a man met him and greeted him with these words . . ." The rav turned for a moment to Shlomo: "Hand me a *siddur* for a minute." Opening the prayer book in which the story was reprinted, he turned quickly to the page and read aloud.

"Gentlemen, the man greeted Rabbi Yosé with these words: 'Rabbi, from what place are you? And Rabbi Yosé answered him: 'I come from a great city of sages and scholars.' And the man replied: 'Rabbi, are you willing to live with us in our place? I will give you a million golden dinars, and precious stones and pearls.' And do you know, gentlemen, what Rabbi Yosé answered him?"

That was my cue, and as if I were sitting at my parents' table once again, I recited the reply: "Yes—he said: 'Were you to give me all the silver and gold and precious stones and pearls in the world, I would not live anywhere except in a place of Torah.'"

"Precisely." The rav smiled, and he and all the others in the room looked at me.

"Your Hebrew is excellent. Where did you learn it?"

"In America."

"So! How is it possible? With your accent, you speak and sound like a native."

"I am a Jew, and Hebrew is our language."

"But not all Jews speak Hebrew well."

"Shmulik is not like all Jews," Ian answered, and patted me on the knee under the table.

"You know, gentlemen"—the rav turned once again to the others, but he kept looking back at me—"all day I teach many classes—that's a part of my job in the Ministry." Like all other professional rabbis in Israel, he was nominally an employee of the Ministry of Religion, assigned a parish and exercising rabbinic responsibilities within it. "But when I come here on Tuesday nights, to Reb Shlomo's *bes medresh*, and I see all of you here so eager to study our holy Torah, so ready to carry out this dearest commandment, I stop being an official and I become one of you, seeking to carry out God's sacred will, studying His holy Torah. Here I can feel at home, because here I am not an outsider helping you fulfill the commandment to study. Here I am one of you, fulfilling that commandment along with you."

Shlomo fidgeted in his seat, stretched his neck and adjusted his tie. This was a testimonial to his success as the group's organizer. *"Baruch ha-Shem, baruch ha-Shem,"* he said, blessing God but seeming to praise himself more.

The rav cut him off. *"Tanya,"* he began, reading aloud from the text. It was enough to get us all to immediately focus upon the text open before us. "Abba Binyamin said: 'There are two things I have fretted about all my life—that I pray before I die and that I lie with my body lying north to south.'

"What does this mean, the *Gemara* asks—that his death be put off by his prayers or that he have an opportunity to pray just before his death?"

A few of the men tried to cue the text and began to offer an answer, but the rav continued with his reading. "It means that he hoped for the opportunity to pray just before the moment of his passing.

"And what does it mean to lie with his body lying north to south?"

Here was the Talmud in its exquisite transparency and opacity—all in one text. First came a profound message that all people could comprehend: a man wanted to pray before his death, but the anxiety of that death troubled and consumed him all his days. But then came a message about how to lie in bed that was at best shrouded in mystery and at worst steeped in superstition. I started to remember all my misgivings about the Talmud and its ways. But the rav was ahead of me.

"Gentlemen. This is not an easy piece of *Gemara*. We must struggle to give it meaning."

The struggle to give meaning to a sacred text—that perhaps more than anything else reflected the devotion of the men of the *bes medresh*. To discover meaning even where there appears to be little; to dismiss nothing of the sacred tradition.

The rav continued: "We have learned a law that people are not too careful about these days—to place their beds along a north–south line. But we must discover why this is so. First, though, let us go back to the beginning of the text.

" 'All my life I have fretted.' Why must he fret?"

"A good question," the man across from me remarked.

The rav continued: "I ask you, gentlemen, why must he fret?

It could, of course, mean that he 'took care.' But it says that he 'fretted.' Well, we can understand why he fretted. After all, which of us can know what it will be like just before we die? It must surely cause us all a deep anxiety. Lying in a bed facing north and south—that's something else. What's there to fret about? What's so difficult? You turn your bed around and it's done.

"But the matter is not simple. A man is a complex creation, made up of a body and a soul, forces that oppose each other—like fire and water. If a person leads them both according to the ways of the Torah, then the soul can be carried and controlled by the body. As water fills a physical form, so the soul may be poured into its shape by a body that carries it in the way of Torah.

"Prayer bears the soul. It is not, gentlemen, simply the recitation of words. It *bears the soul*—that is what the beginning of our text is trying to tell us." His inflection implored our understanding; his loud voice demanded it. "As the bed bears the body, Abba Binyamin wanted his soul and his body to be under the sway of the Torah, for he understood that the two were intertwined, inseparable."

For a few moments the Talmud had been opened up, and I could see into a text that a moment earlier had been opaque to me. Through metaphor, the rabbi had taken all of us into a passage that would otherwise have excluded me. That literary approach was something I could relate to and comprehend. It could bridge my two worlds. This way of *lernen* was more exciting than what I had witnessed at Shaarey Chesed. There I had only observed in awe as my partners faithfully cracked their way into the page. Here I could enter with everyone around me, for their Talmudic reasoning and my own fitted together. We had moved in Heichal Baruch away from the literalism of Shaarey Chesed or the mysticism of Bratslav and Menachem.

The men around me had remained silently attentive as the rav offered his explication of the text, but I let my attention flag as I read through the text and tried to mentally reconstruct the argument and poetry of what I had just heard. To *lern* on my own, I had to be able to review whatever I had been taught. Suddenly there was a rumble of conversation. It jarred me loose from my thoughts and I tuned in to the teacher again. By now the subject had changed.

The conversation had turned to tracing the law that demanded a man pray as close to the wall as is possible. From the philosophical flights of reasoning with which we had begun, we now looped into and out of legal arguments, trying to straighten out the law and discover its demands. Some asked questions; others offered challenges or alternative interpretations. It dawned on me that by now we were reenacting in our *lernen* precisely what the text itself was doing: jumping from topic to topic, story to story, debate to debate. That was what it meant to enter into the Talmud, to speak its words as if they were one's own. We were giving life to the Oral Tradition that had been embedded in the pages in front of us.

Throughout the time, I tried to listen and comprehend. And always while I whispered the texts and tried to stamp into my memory what I had learned, the subject would change and people would be talking about another law or telling another story.

The rav was not just reciting the Talmud we studied; he was almost singing it. His voice rose and fell and brought a new life to the words. "Rabbi Hanina said in the name of Rav: 'Anyone who reviews the Talmud without singing it, without intoning its words, has not reviewed the sacred laws I have given him.'"

I was not yet ready to sing out the words, but perhaps I would be able to do so soon. I thought of a Hasidic story Yosef Moshe Reichler had told me on my last visit. The disciples of Reb Baruch of Mezibizh, one of the early followers of the Baal Shem

Tov, once asked him: "How can a man ever learn the Talmud adequately? We have but little pieces of what the great sages said to one another. How can we fully enter into their debates?" And their rebbe answered them: "You must link your soul to the souls of those sages. That is what is meant in the Talmud when we read that when a word is spoken in the name of its speaker, his lips move in the grave. The lips of him who utters the words move like those of the master who is dead."

Reb Shimileh was bringing in tea and cookies now. During the early part of the hour he had been sitting in a corner with tape and scissors repairing the bindings of old holy books while the tea was being brewed. But although he could not follow the words of the text, he had learned to read the tempo and rhythm of the *lernen*. He heard the slow warming up, the questions and answers, cues and echoes, debates and digressions. And he heard when we reached the climax of the hour and when after that dramatic moment our attention began slowly to flag. Once, when I asked him just how he knew when to serve the tea, he smiled and said, "I hear it in the voices, see it in the faces and feel it in the room."

The rav got his tea first, a glass filled with the darkest liquid of all, a bag still in it. Then each of the others got one. I didn't know it then, but I would later learn that there was a precise order in the way the drinks were distributed. The scholars and seniors were first; young newcomers like me came last.

At first the tea party seemed to me extraneous to the *lernen*. In the interstices of an argument someone would whisper a request for the cookie plate or sugar bowl. Between the flights of narrative and legalistic argument the sounds of spoons stirring sugar into glasses seemed incidental.

But when I saw, week after week, how important the ritual of its distribution and drinking was to the men, I began to wonder if I was missing some of its significance. Never would the group allow the tea to be missed. Never would they even permit it to come too late. And when once or twice Reb Shimileh was absent, no less a one than Shlomo himself took up the task of preparing and serving it—often at the rav's urging. But although I came to look forward to the tea as much as all the others, it wasn't until I reviewed my tape recordings of this first visit that I finally saw the connection. It was in the relationship between body and the spirit. One might refresh the spirit with Talmud, but precisely because—as the rav told us on my first night—the body and soul were forces opposing each other, one could not refresh one without sustaining the other. Our hearts might be warmed by words of Torah, but our bodies also needed a hot tea. And besides, men who traveled together through the special world of the page shared a fellowship that the tea helped cement.

That was where Reb Shimileh fitted into the picture; he brought the tea. But in that he did more than it might seem. He who faithfully serves scholars, the Talmud explains, gains all the merit of their learning.

After that first evening, I became a regular at Heichal Baruch. As the weeks and months passed, I found myself looking forward all week to my Tuesday-evening class. The rav was beginning to ask me questions, and I found myself preparing for them in advance. I too had questions to ask. More and more I was entering the *lernen*. In the give-and-take of the class, the Talmud had become for me something more than simply a book; it had taken on the vitality of the Oral Tradition from which it sprang. Tuesday nights before class, I would repeat the words of the text aloud as I reviewed them at home. The Talmud was becoming for me a cultural transmitter, and I was

more and more able to pick up its signals and move along its
wavelength.

In time I established a place for myself inside the circle. The
little tape recorder with which I captured every lesson became a
key to my membership. My tapes would contain the unbroken
record of the group's progress. Every so often I would play a
few minutes of a previous class session or lend someone a cas-
sette to listen to at home. The recordings, the rav cautioned me,
must never be erased. They were endowed with a sanctity far
beyond anything any of us could imagine, for they contained
the holiest words of the Oral Tradition. And I had become its
guardian.

While I was a part of the circle, my enthusiasm for *lernen*
burned. But I could not help wondering if this fire would remain
when I was on my own, for although I did not know exactly
when the time would come for me to leave Heichal Baruch, I
had no doubt it would. A life was still waiting for me back in the
United States and in the university, and sooner or later I knew I
would have to return to it. Before that time, I needed some
assurance that I would leave Jerusalem in possession of this
flame.

One evening, as the rav was reviewing the closing lines of the
volume we had been studying during all the time I had been in
the circle, something happened that was to help me gain some of
the assurance I had been awaiting. The *siyum*, the celebration
of the end of a portion of our study, was at hand, and a kind of
electricity was in the air. We were completing more than a
book; we were turning a corner of our lives. Rabbi Rotenbush
read aloud the wisdom of the great sage Rabbi Yochanan:

"Anyone who grasps the Torah without its mantle will be
buried without his mantle."

I had long since ceased dismissing opaque Talmudic dicta as

beyond my comprehension. Words, phrases and ideas that seemed unintelligible could be penetrated. And when we managed to interpret our way through such a text, those were the moments of highest intellectual and emotional drama. They were times during which all of us seemed held close to the ancients.

"Could this mean that someone who simply touched the scroll without a mantle on it would be buried without a shroud?" someone asked.

"No," through the rav's voice, and in dialogue with us, the Talmud replied, "it simply means that one is buried naked—that is, bereft—of the benefit of good deeds."

"Could that really be the case?"

"Could the law be so extreme over such a small transgression?"

"No," the rabbis explained, "one is buried naked, unadorned by the fulfillment of that one commandment: to be circumspect when approaching the holy Torah scroll."

Step by step we were cutting into the Talmud's logic. But as we did so, it was clear that we had not yet reached the core of the idea. Each question and answer echoed louder than the last; each led us forward to some solution at which we could rest.

We began to mumble among ourselves, trying to temper the text to our own understanding of our Judaism.

"This can't be all there is." "Could the *Gemara* be so simple?" "Why do the rabbis make so much of this?"

The rav cut us all short. "Let us enter into the heart of the idea, gentlemen. We know that the Master of the Universe made a covenant with us at Sinai. The Talmud tells us"—he cited chapter and verse—"that the covenant was not simply what we read in the Scriptures but included as well the Oral Tradition.

"The Scriptures are not so easily understood, gentlemen. They are abbreviated, packed with hints and secret meanings.

But the Oral Tradition"—and by this we all knew he meant the Talmud, in which that tradition had been deposited by the sages —"the Oral Tradition is the mantle of the Torah."

His voice had softened; the men leaned back in their seats. We knew we were entering a new level of understanding. Now we would plunge into the great commentaries.

"When God gave us the Torah at Sinai He held the mountain over our heads."

The teacher addressed us as if we ourselves had been present at Sinai. According to the tradition, we had been, for all generations—past and future—took part in the covenant.

"But how can it be that he held a mountain as a threat above our heads? We know that we accepted the Torah willingly: 'We shall do and we shall listen.' "

Everyone around the table knew the line, the faithful response by which our forebears and we their children had accepted the Torah even before we knew what it contained: "We shall do" before "we shall listen."

"So how can our sages tell us that God held the mountain over our heads, warning us that if we did not accept His Torah He would bury us there at Sinai?"

This was no idle or theoretical question in the way that it was being asked now. It had all the urgency of a personal quandary. The rav turned us to the column on the outside of our page. "Shmulik, can you give us the answer?"

There was a time I would have had nothing to say, when I could not have brought myself to speak for the Talmud. But that time was over, and now I knew it. I plunged into the commentary and excerpted it for all of us: "The commentaries of the Tosphot explain that he who does not learn the Oral Tradition will be buried by the dense weight of Scripture." I thought for a moment of my attachment to Scripture and how I was now ready to move beyond it. And then I continued: "If we listen only to the condensed words of the written Torah, if we do not surround it with the mantle of the Oral Tradition, if we do not *lern* the *Gemara,* here shall we be buried. We cannot comprehend the full meanings of each verse of the Bible, we cannot fathom its depths without the light of the Talmud. Without it we are like the dead; you are as good as buried. That, gentlemen, is what is meant when Rabbi Yochanan says that if we try to grasp the Torah without its mantle *we* shall be buried without our mantle."

The room was silent. I turned red.

"Terrific!" Ian whispered to me in English.

"A scholar," Shlomo said chuckling; "he can *lern.*"

The rav smiled and picked up the threads of the argument again.

"If you do not accept My Torah, then and there will you be buried." He read from the Talmud.

"But where is 'there'?" he asked. "There, among all the nations of the world, from whom you will be no different. For if you have not put on the mantle of the Talmud, you will understand the Scripture as do all other nations; you will be like them. The Talmud, gentlemen, is our Jewishness; it is our mark of distinction, the emblem of our understanding. We do not *lern Gemara* simply to acquire knowledge; we do it to preserve our Jewish lives."

I declined Ian's offer of a ride home that night and walked instead. I wanted to play back in my mind the events of the evening. I had made a breakthrough: reviewing a complex piece of the Talmud for the class. This new step was not, however, completely unexpected. It seemed rather a confirmation of what had been going on for quite a while. Over the months at Heichal Baruch, and perhaps even before, I had been coming ineluctably closer to *lernen* and the Talmud. I had experienced that closeness only after confronting the possibility of my "going stranger." Only then, perhaps, had I been ready to find a group of men who like me could see beyond the literal meanings of the text.

The men around me had made a living symbol of the Talmud and used metaphor to connect themselves to its Jewish wisdom. The words and phrases—the legalisms and narratives—were, in their deepest structure, expressions of Jewish consciousness and affirmations of traditional culture. Before this evening, the night on which we were about to complete our first volume of the Talmud, I had never joined publicly in that act of expression and affirmation. Tonight, at last, I had come out in public— completed my initiation—and begun to *lern* Talmud on my own. And the verse I had chosen for my display of *lernen* was one that helped me at last to articulate the tie that Talmud had to my life as a Jew.

I had for years failed to understand the true nature of Judaism, both as religious Jew and as sociologist, because I had not understood the Talmudic process and its significance. The Talmud was the central symbol of my cultural heritage, essential to the Jew in me, in all my people. "We do not *lern Gemara* simply to acquire knowledge; we do it to preserve our Jewish lives." The rav's remark was crucial. It punctuated my performance.

But, I wondered as I walked, did this mean I had to comprehend the Talmud in only one way? If I did, would I not be once again in the same situation of conflict with my modernity as I had been before coming to Heichal Baruch?

"There are six hundred thousand aspects and meanings of the Torah," wrote Menachem Azariah da Fano, the sixteenth-century Italian kabbalist; and he continued: "according to each one of these ways of explaining the Torah, the root of a soul has been fashioned in Israel."

I had come to the Talmud circle as a participant-observer and for a time had lost my status as participant. Now I had it back again. My *lernen* could be at once both a religious exercise—a *mitzva*—and a way to reenact, exhibit, discover and reinforce my ties to my people—a kind of performance of Jewish culture. By entering the *chavruse*, I could *act like a Jew*. With his interpretation of the page, the rav had as much as said that afterward. Through *lernen*, I had been preserving the Jewishness of my life.

But did this mean there was no room left for the sociologist in me? I knew I was not going to spend the rest of my days in *lernen*. What, then, was I going to take away from these experiences I had had?

The next day, soon after I awoke, I turned on my tape recorder and began at last reviewing all the tapes I had collected. With each, I opened the pertinent pages and volumes. And thus I sat, surrounded by the Talmud and ensconced in its review. Gradually, I found my own way of disambiguating and opening up the text. It required my thinking about what I was reviewing not just as a Jew but also as a sociologist and anthropologist. Passages in the Talmud were being completed in my mind with ideas from the literature of my profession which helped me understand not only what the Talmud was saying but what the men who *lernt* it were doing. Only thus—with a double vision, a parallax view—could I see through the text into my peoplehood.

As I listened to the tapes, I realized that the groups I had joined had helped me in my sentimental education, allowing me to discover the fundamental spirit and character of my Judaism along with my responses to it. When we reviewed the passages and ideas inside this timeless book, we were at the same time making sense of the events through which we and our Jewish forebears passed. We stamped into our consciousness the traditional patterns of Jewish life which the pages we studied celebrated. Those truths became ours, if only during the time of our *lernen*. Others might share our Scriptures, but only we, the

Jews, had the mantle. I saw the mantle as a social scientist, but it was as a Jew that I wanted to put it on.

The hours passed swiftly, as I immersed myself in the sounds and memories of months of classes. The process of *lernen* Talmud was like an inkblot: each participant could see in it what was meaningful to him as a Jew. As I relived the moments of my *lernen*, I began to see and hear things I had remained unaware of at the time—just as I had done on that first occasion when I listened to my tapes of Shaarey Chesed. In one tape, I discovered an example of a religious drama, as the men tried to come to terms with a redundant passage and argued over their varying interpretations of a holy text. In another, there was an episode in which we entered into Jewish tradition and brought it forward into our own time. At that session we spent more time getting ideas off our chests than putting the words of the Talmud into our hearts. But all the time we were *lernen*, we seemed to be discovering our Jewish being through the open page of a holy book.

And then, as I reviewed more of the tapes, I noticed how the social context in which the *lernen* occurred was in many ways as important as the substance of the study itself, for it was an opportunity for us all to express our solidarity with one another and through them the Jewish people.

We came together to *lern*, but our coming together was as important a part of what we did as the *lernen* itself. That, after all, was why the tea and cookies and Reb Shimileh mattered so much to everyone at Heichal Baruch, why we danced at Bratslav or shared food around Rav Krol's table. *Lernen*, in fact, seemed always to take place around tables where all of us could face one another. The Jewish circle would not be broken; *lernen* would keep all who engaged in it in the great chain of Jewish being.

These were perhaps not the meanings the men in the circles

I joined gave to their *lernen*, but they were the ways I found to make the experience meaningful. I re-*lernt* all I could in my own terms. Surrounded by the Talmud, I was thinking in the analytic perspective of my discipline. The two sets of books on my shelf were now at last together; the two worlds were meeting, and I sat between them. When I looked up, I saw that it was nearly dark.

But I felt no desire to stop. Like Reb Zusya of Hanipol, I had found the place from which I felt no need to escape. Not until today had I ever spent a full day *lernen*. Never could I thus have sustained my interest and involvement. A day had come and gone, and I sat over my volumes of Talmud. Perhaps I had at last repaired myself to study Torah; perhaps I had found a way to pass between the kingdom of Esau and that of Jacob.

I stopped to eat a quick supper and then took the bus to Shaarey Chesed. I would be just in time for the *lernen* with my old *chavruse*. After spending the whole day alone with the Talmud, I needed some fellowship. More than that, I wanted to know if I had changed, if my way of listening to the Talmud would still allow me to be in a *chavruse* where people heard it in other ways.

This time I took bus number nine back into the world of *lernen* and not to the university. But this trip was different, for I needed no escape to a refuge on the mountain.

"Blessed is He who revives the dead," Rav Moses greeted me. If he only knew how good it felt to hear that blessing recited over me. It had been months since I had joined my old partners in *lernen*. Someone handed me a pinch of snuff as I slid into my old place. I was in. I felt a fresh confidence and enthusiasm. I was ready to *lern* tonight as never before.

The Talmud we reviewed that evening dealt, as usual, with the matter of what was an appropriate and what a spoiled Temple sacrifice. The text was, in fact, a kind of running commen-

tary on an array of verses from the book of Leviticus. One by
one it analyzed and ordered the archaic practices and long-
neglected rituals the Scriptures described. The sacrifices were to
be offered upon the mountain where the Holy Temple stood.

Someone quoted a verse from Psalms. "Who shall ascend the
mount of the Lord? He that has clean hands and a pure heart."

The worshiper who partakes of the sacrifice, Rav Moses explained, sits at the table of the Lord. He who brought the
sacrifice, Reb Yechiel Michl added, had to bring with it a re-
newed faith, as if each time he sat at the Lord's table he were
performing the rite for the first time in his life.

That which we may have performed in the past, I thought, we
are not free to forget.

In my new frame of mind, this sort of *lernen* was a kind of
spiritual exercise. Replaying the sacrifices through our repetition of the laws concerning them was a way to demonstrate
continued faith in God and Jewish peoplehood. Perhaps that
was behind these men's literalness, their concern with every jot
and tittle of the ceremony. Perhaps that was what enabled them
to see the sacrifices to which I had remained blind. With this
reasoning, I could, if I tried, join the others in trying to get the
laws straight and ceremonies clear. After all, how different was
such a spiritual exercise from the one I engaged in when I
prayed side by side with these men or with the Hasidim of
Bratslav? I tried to orient my spirit to the page as did the men
around me, to feel at home.

What swept me up now, as it had before at Heichal Baruch,
was the vision of men becoming Jews by reviewing Talmud. It
was not just the Jew in me that was stimulated by the occasion,
however. It was also a tremendously exciting occurrence to
watch as an anthropologist. And so I displayed the same level of
involvement as those men near me. I repeated words, nodded
my comprehension, asked questions—all in order to feel what it

meant to thereby become a Jew. While it may have been participant-observer fervor which fired me as a Jew—something different from what energized the people around me—that still got me further into the action than had ever been possible here before when I could only watch.

"You've been *lernen* on your own?" Reb Asher asked as we walked out that night. For the first time he had spoken to me directly. I looked at him and smiled. He nodded back.

On Thursday morning, I went back to Mintzer's. All the books I had selected there on my first visit sat on my shelf, new and hardly ever touched. They had made my library grow. They were all commentaries on the Bible and its contents. But I knew now that "if you have not put on the mantle of the Talmud, you will understand the Scripture as do all other nations; you will be like them." It was time to get a new set of books.

To my surprise, the Mintzers remembered me. I asked to go to the storeroom.

"I have been having a little difficulty breathing and find it hard to go up and down the stairs more than once a day," Mr. Mintzer said. "If you don't mind, please take the key and go on down yourself. Spend as much time as you need."

I walked down the narrow stairwell and into the cellar. At the bottom, I opened the door and turned on the light. The smell of fresh bindings and musty pages filled my nostrils. My eyes fell at once upon the wall of Talmuds before me. Ready to scale it, I walked over to the shelf and ran my fingers over the bindings. They drummed themselves across the thirty volumes. I slid my hand from one shelf to another until it stopped at the Steinsaltz editions.

Adin Steinsaltz was a young Israeli who, like me, had once confronted the world of *lernen* as an outsider. Now he had mastered it. Halfway between the *bes medresh* and the university, he was capable of reviewing any volume of Talmud with all the attachment of a pious Jew. Yet he could also be asked, as he had been, to give the prestigious Terry Lectures at Yale. With a new edition of the text, he had found a way to enable modern students to enter the immemorial, complex world of the Talmud. Taking the ancient telegraphic, almost cryptic Aramaic writings, Steinsaltz had provided a running commentary and modern Hebrew translation of them in the margins. The task was far from complete; only about fifteen volumes of the Talmud were done. But with those editions already prepared, a novice like me could make his way through the pages with Steinsaltz and the modern world at his side. I piled the books into my arms and went upstairs.

"I see you're getting set to do some serious studying," Mrs. Mintzer said as I paid her for the set of books. "That man has opened up the Talmud for a whole new generation of scholars. Now you will join them."

As I left Mintzer's with my books in a brown wrapper, I made my way to Mea Shearim and the Reichlers'. I hadn't seen them in a while, and somehow a visit now felt appropriate. The walk was not a long one, but carrying the books made it seem longer. The rough hemp that Mintzer had used to tie them together was already starting to cut into my palms.

I knocked on the door, and it was opened by Menachem. Stunned for a moment, I said nothing. I hadn't seen him since he had sent me off for repair. But he recognized me this time and let me inside.

"I came to visit your parents."

"They will be home soon. My mother took my father to the doctor."

"Is he all right?"

"With God's help. He needed some medicine for the flu."

He looked at my package.

"Steinsaltz," I said.

"Have you found it possible to *lern*, then?" he asked.

"I think so, but I still need help."

"And Steinsaltz will be that help?"

"He and my *chavruse*."

Just then the door opened and the senior Reichlers walked in. Mrs. Reichler greeted me warmly while she helped her husband take off his coat. As usual he was out of breath. Menachem took the coat and hat from her and put them in the bedroom.

"Tea?" she asked. "I'm making some anyway."

"*Nu?*" Reb Yosef Moshe crinkled his eyes at me. It was his way of asking me to talk about myself.

"I've been to Mintzer's again."

"More books?" he wheezed.

"I've bought Steinsaltz."

"So!" He inclined his head, and Menachem sat down across from him.

"What do you think of our scholar?" Reb Yosef Moshe asked him.

"Let's hear what you have been *lernen*," Menachem said, a slight edge of cynicism in his voice.

"*Nu*, which tractate?" his father added, pointing his son toward the bookcase.

I sent them to the volume I had been studying and reviewed the discussion of the mantle and the Torah. The text was by now quite familiar, but at first I couldn't help feeling a bit anxious as I went over it for them. I had seen Reb Yosef Moshe listen to his grandchildren review their studies for him when they visited on the Sabbath. Now that he was watching me in the same way, I felt like them. But as I grew more and more possessed by what I was doing, my anxiety seemed to melt away.

The time passed quickly, and the three of us became involved in a full-blown session of study. The tea was brought and then Mrs. Reichler tiptoed into the bedroom, closing the door behind her. The sound of our recitations and discussion filled the small room. Occasionally, the father or son would offer a gloss on one point or another or ask me to amplify some aspect of the argument. And then Reb Yosef Moshe offered insights from one of the many commentaries on the text that I did not know. But throughout I remained the *maggid shiur,* the one who led the class. It was I who recited the text and tried to keep the thread of Talmudic reasoning from becoming twisted.

When I had finished, Reb Yosef Moshe spoke first.

"Do you remember what I told you about people who are possessed by their books?"

I nodded.

"I was afraid that you were much more interested in acquiring a library than in becoming possessed. And when I saw you today and you told me that you had bought more books, I worried that you were still afflicted with this acquisitive disease. I think Menachem was wondering too."

Menachem said nothing.

"But now that I have heard you, I am no longer worried."

He was right about one thing: I had become possessed. I told him how I had spent the day *lernen* and how the night before my mind had become caught up with what I had reviewed, as if all I had been through had suddenly and finally exploded into my consciousness.

"Rabbi Hannania ben Yaakov tells us," he said, laughing, "that if one is kept awake in the night by words of Torah, it is a good sign. Do not worry that you have become so possessed. It is a blessing, for the Torah is 'a tree of life to those who grasp it.'"

"But not without a mantle," I added. Reb Yosef Moshe laughed again, and I did too.

Hearing our laughter, Mrs. Reichler opened the door and entered.

"Finished?" she asked.

"A pause," her husband answered. "There's never a finish as long as we live and breathe—only a pause."

He was right again. I had embarked upon a path that had no end. There would be crossroads when I moved from one *chavruse* to another, when I followed one line of study or another, when I returned to my life in the university. But there was no end in sight. I had the entire Talmud and Jewish tradition before me. I would not enter completely into it, but at least I now could stand at the gate.

Reb Yosef Moshe was getting tired, and I stood up to leave. Menachem was going too. We walked through the courtyard together, but soon I fell a few steps behind; I was still weighed down by my bundle of books. As the hemp began to cut into my hand again, I wondered silently if I hadn't taken on too much, if I would really continue to *lern* from all these volumes after this day. And while I thought about this possibility that my time in the *bes medresh* might be limited by who I was and where I might be going, Menachem led me out of the streets of his world as if he knew that I could not and would not stay there. He said nothing and looked straight ahead, but he walked slowly enough so that I could just about keep up with him. With Menachem in front, we crossed Mea Shearim Street and climbed a few steps that took us into a maze of alleys which in turn opened into a narrow and deserted passage that wound it way around the back of a row of houses. In all my visits to the Reichlers, I had not ever left this way. Turning a corner, we suddenly found ourselves near the end of the lane and just short of the center of town. Menachem stopped, as if he were approaching some invisible border. Instinctively, I stopped too.

For the first time since we had left his father's house he turned toward me. He looked into my eyes and spoke to me as if he had been reading my thoughts, and as though I knew he had.

As he spoke, his voice solemnly quiet, I felt as if he were at once pleased by my progress and wary of it.

"A scholar once came to a great rebbe. The scholar was no longer young—he was close to thirty—but he had never before visited a rebbe. 'What have you done all your life?' the rebbe asked him. 'I have gone through the whole of the Talmud three times,' the learned man answered. 'Yes,' the rebbe replied, and then inquired, 'but how much of the Talmud has gone through you?'"

Menachem paused and then stretched out his hand to shake mine. He had never touched me before. "According to the effort is the reward," he said, and walked away.

GLOSSARY

Ark: A small closet or chamber in the synagogue in which the holy Torah scrolls are commonly stored.

Baal Shem Tov: Israel ben Eliezer, eighteenth-century founder of Hasidism, born in Eastern Europe and grandfather of Rabbi Nahman of Bratslav.

bes medresh: House of Jewish study.

bimah: Pulpit on which the Torah scroll is placed while being read. Commonly located in the center of the men's section of the synagogue. Sometimes prayers are led from here as well.

biryoni: Zealots, especially those who organized a revolt against the Romans around the year 70 C.E.

cantor: The person who formally leads or chants the prayers in the synagogue service.

chavruse: Fellowship of *lerners*, or students engaged in the review of Jewish (usually Talmudic) texts.

daven: Pray.

gabbai: The man responsible for the dispensing of ritual tasks and generally in charge of the conduct of prayer services in the synagogue.

gaon: A genius, particularly in matters of Jewish scholarship.

Gemara (also *Gemore*): A portion of the Talmud, the so-called "completion" of the *Mishna* (the basis of the Talmud, which traces its origins to an oral tradition with roots at Sinai and the divine revelation there), as developed in the Jewish scholarly academies of Babylonia and Palestine [Israel]. A record of the oral debate and discussion among the sages that is neither concise nor systematic in its treatment of subjects. Often used colloquially as a synonym for Talmud.

gemore-nign: Talmudic chant, a singsong whose rising and falling cadences help to disambiguate the sometimes cryptic and abbreviated texts.

ha-Shem: The Name—a traditional Jewish way of referring to God.

Hasid: A follower of the way of the Baal Shem Tov; an adherent of Hasidism.

kabbala: Jewish mysticism.

Kaddish: The Aramaic prayer of praise recited by a male relative in response to the death of a kinsman. It is recited in the synagogue during the morning, afternoon and evening prayers for the first eleven months following bereavement and then afterward on the anniversary of the death.

Kotel: Literally, a wall. Commonly refers to the western wall of the ancient Holy Temple in Jerusalem, most of which still stands today and which has become perhaps one of the holiest sites of Judaism.

lebedik: Lively.

lernen: The eternal review and ritualized study of sacred Jewish texts.

ma'ariv: The evening prayer.

maggid: A narrator. Commonly one who tells stories and through them offers Jewish moral and religious instruction.

Marrano: A term of opprobrium used to denigrate New Christians of Spain and Portugal of the fifteenth and sixteenth centuries. Most probably derived from the Spanish word meaning "swine." Often Marranos secretly continued to practice aspects of their Judaism, and thus the term has come to denote those who secretly observe Judaism even as they appear to be non-Jewish.

Masada: One of King Herod's royal citadels and the last outpost of the Zealots [*biryoni*] during the Jewish war against Rome around the year 73 C.E. Situated atop an isolated rock on the edge of the Judean desert and Dead Sea valley, it was taken after a lengthy siege by the Romans. But the Zealot defenders committed mass suicide rather than surrender.

menorah: A candelabrum. The seven-branched *menorah* built and placed in the Holy Temple is the most famous and the one from which the term is derived.

mezuza: Literally a doorpost, this term has come to refer to the small parchment on which are inscribed certain scriptural verses and which by Jewish law is to be placed on the right side of doorways.

midrash: A method used to bring out lessons through stories or homily. It is as well the designation of a particular genre of rabbinic literature which mixes Biblical exegesis with homily. Often the term simply connotes legend.

mikveh: A ritual bath; commonly used by women seven days after the end of their menstrual cycle but also by men before Sabbaths and holy days and for the purification of newly acquired dishes. The water in the *mikveh* must flow from a natural source—one with no chemical additives.

mincha: The afternoon prayer.

minyan: Literally, "number"; commonly refers to the quorum of ten or more men necessary for the convening of communal prayer. It must, among the Orthodox, consist of males over the age of thirteen. While others may participate in the service, only adult Jewish males are counted in the *minyan*.

Mishna: Codification of basic Jewish law, redacted and arranged by Rabbi Judah ha-Nasi circa 200 C.E. It contains an Oral Law transmitted through generations and is the nucleus of the Talmud.

Mishna Brura: One of the classic codices of Jewish law.

mitzva: Religious obligation; sometimes a synonym for "righteous act."

parshan, parshanim (pl.): Commentator (s).

peya, peyos (pl.): Earlocks, commonly worn by Hasidim.

rab, rabbi, rav, reb, rebbe: A variety of terms for rabbi. The last (rebbe) is commonly reserved for Hasidic rabbinic leaders.

Rambam: Acronym for Maimonides, a twelfth-century Jewish philosopher, exegete, codifier, commentator and physician.

shadchan: Jewish matchmaker.

Shalom aleichem: Literally "Peace be unto you," it is a common form of Jewish greeting, to which the normal reply is the inversion: "Aleichem shalom."

SHaS: A popular name for the Talmud; an acronym for the Hebrew expression "*Shisha Sedarim*," denoting the "six orders," or categories, into which the Talmud is divided.

sefer, seforim (pl.): Book(s); commonly refers to religious or scholarly books written in Hebrew, Aramaic or occasionally Yiddish and pertaining to Jewish matters.

shtender: A small lectern, often used during *lernen* or prayer, inside which a small library of Jewish texts may be stored.

shtibble, shtibblach (pl.): A small, intimate chamber which serves as a house of prayer, study and assembly.

talis: A ritually fringed four-cornered garment normally worn by adult males during prayer.

talis koton: A small, ritually fringed four-cornered garment worn by Orthodox Jewish males whenever they are dressed. Some males wear the garment so that the fringes are visible, while others keep it entirely under their shirt and out of sight.

Talmud: A compendium of Oral Law (the *Mishna*), together with notes of rabbinic analysis, discussion and commentary (the *Gemara*).

t'filin: Phylacteries. Small leather box-shaped chambers which contain excerpts of Scripture written on parchment and which are placed on the head and left arm of adult Jewish males during the recitation of weekday-morning prayers.

Torah: The corpus of Jewish law, lore and rabbinic commentary which is the central organizing element of Jewish religion and tradition and which is considered by believers to be divinely inspired and revealed. The term is sometimes used also to refer to the scroll on which the Five Books of Moses are inscribed and

from which Jews regularly chant portions during their prayer
services.

Tosaphot: Literally, "additions." Collections of comments on the Talmud, generally based upon and glosses of earlier commentaries.

tzedake: Charity.

tzitzis: Ritually knotted fringes which are placed on all four-cornered
garments in accordance with the injunction in Numbers 15:37–
41.

yarmulke (also *kippah*): A skullcap.

yeshiva: An academy of higher or advanced Jewish learning.

zaddik: A righteous man.

ACKNOWLEDGMENTS

Throughout these pages I have been bound by the facts of my experience. Certain sequences of events, however, have been changed or shortened to make the narrative flow more smoothly. In some cases, the people described in this book have been given pseudonyms to protect their privacy. I wish to thank them and those whose real names appear for having graciously allowed me to join with them in their *lernen*. Without their willingness to open their circles to me, my life would have been significantly impoverished and I could not have written this book. My wife, Ellin, from the beginning and until today, remains a constant source of encouragement as well as my best critic. Without the example and urging of my rabbi, Psachya Weinberger, I would never have begun. I feel privileged to know him. Finally, my editor, Arthur H. Samuelson, encouraged me to go to the limits of my ability to tell my story. I thank him for helping me find within myself the resources I needed to finish what I had begun.

As the rabbis have written: "Who is wise? He who learns from all others."

SAMUEL HEILMAN
New Rochelle, New York

ABOUT THE AUTHOR

Samuel Heilman is a professor of sociology at Queens College of the City University of New York and is the author of *Synagogue Life* and *The People of the Book*. Born in Germany and raised in Brookline, Massachusetts, he now lives with his wife, Ellin, and their four sons, Adam, Uriel, Avram and Jonah, in New Rochelle, New York.